MONTANA'S
BOB MARSHALL COUNTRY

The Bob Marshall, Scapegoat, Great Bear Wilderness Areas and Surrounding Wildlands

Gateway Gorge above Gateway Creek leading to Big River Meadows. Rick Graetz photo.

by Rick Graetz, Publisher,

Montana Magazine, Inc.   Helena, Montana 1985

Andrew Posewitz fishing in the Dearborn River.
Rick Graetz photo.

Front Cover Photo: The Chinese Wall looking south from above Larch Hill Pass. Rick Graetz photo.

Back Cover Photo: Six-year-old Todd Graetz on the trail along the South Fork of the Sun River. Rick Graetz photo

Published by Rick Graetz, Publisher
Montana Magazine, Inc.
Box 5630
Helena, MT 59604

ISBN 0-938314-15-7

All pre-press production completed in Helena, Montana. Typesetting by Thurber Printing. Design by Len Visual Design. Printed in Hong Kong by Flying Colors of Beverly Hills.

Table of Contents

Foreword

by Jim Posewitz

Eighty million years ago in what is now western Montana, our planet strained mightily and heaved upward enormous slabs of layered sedimentary rock. Inexorably, these slabs thrust eastward over the vast stillness of the northern plain.

Slowly this migrating mass of rock overcame the forces that mysteriously propelled it, and the often imperceptible eastward thrusting finally ceased. Enormous ramparts of rock stood silently against the flat land to the east. Primordial winds swept the silent land. The raw physical force of creation had put in place a tumbled, rocky mass that, in time, would become known as the Bob Marshall Country.

The hand of the Creator is never still. Even as this mass of rock was sliding eastward, erosive elements chipped at surfaces that defied their every stroke. Time, however, is also marked on mountains. Glaciers descended from frozen peaks leaving icy gouges that captured primitive rivers. Wind and rain swept the raw surfaces; ice sought every crack, wedging rock from rock. Stone by tumbling stone, the harsh landscape took shape. Somewhere in that misty past, a tinge of green was brushed across the rockscape, and life took root upon this uncommon land.

As the earth turned in the sun, plant communities became complex and carpeted the land. Animals followed, and through the millennia, many creatures drew sustenance from this country; only the force of time was permitted to change it.

Man's history is long in this wild country. He trod its slopes and ridges in bare feet, in moccasins, and in boots. He worshiped amid its uncompromised primitive grandeur; he seeks peace and solitude there today. Perhaps in one of his most perceptive moments, man restrained his own boundless appetite for progress, declaring this country from the Rocky Mountain Front up over the Continental Divide, and on to the crest of the Swan Range, a land that will remain as he found it. The first creature approaching this place with the power to change it has, to this date, had the wisdom not to.

The land just described is the Bob Marshall Country. The country is a gift that comes directly from God's creation. The name we have given it comes from an early forester and conservationist who loved wild land more than life. You will meet him in the text of this book.

To find this place, head for the northern Rockies in central Montana. Find the Continental Divide near the small mountain community of Lincoln; and go north. If walking a straight line were either possible or desirable, you would cross another road about 140 miles later. In between, you would have "touched the earth" and, in turn, you would have been touched, by the incomparable American wilderness.

In the protracted battle to protect this place, three wilderness areas have been designated by Congress. Other wild lands around the classified lands are also a part of this country; they have been designated by the elk, the deer, and the grizzly bear.

The formally classified Bob Marshall Wilderness is the heart of this country; it was designated when the Wilderness Act was passed in 1964. The Lincoln Scapegoat Wilderness was added in 1972. The man who made it happen is Cecil Garland. You'll meet him, too, farther down the trail. The Great Bear Wilderness, adjoining the "Bob" on the north, was the latest addition. The late Senator from Montana, Lee Metcalf, secured it for his people in 1978. His story also awaits you.

As this story of the Bob Marshall Country is written, it can be written with pride. The streams run clear, as they always have. Several thousand elk are secure because people care. The bighorn sheep herd is the largest and most significant in the nation because their needs come first in this place. Grizzly bears still pad the deep forest and foothill marshes, unaware that this may be their last stronghold in the lower 48 states. Perhaps most important, this wild country gives substance to one of the noblest concepts of our American culture, the idea of preserving at least a little wild country for the common good of the American people, present and future. It is a concept, born in the robust American pride of things wild, given life by people like Teddy Roosevelt, and honed to a sharp understanding by sensitive philosophers like Aldo Leopold.

Since white men have occupied the west, this wild country has been at the crossroads. There have always been threats to the integrity of its wildness, just as there are threats today. There are always those who want the land, the dam site, the timber, the hidden mineral, the wildlife. Also there always have been men who have cared — and stood in defense of this uncommon place. You will hear from and about Bruce Neal, Dale Burk, Bob Cooney, Nels Thoreson, Hobnail Tom Edwards and others like them — names not as recognizable as Roosevelt, Marshall and Leopold, yet their contributions are just as important to the land and its life.

Each day the pressure increases to compromise the land just consolidated into a wilderness masterpiece. The commodities beyond the boundaries will continue to attract the exploiter. The same overthrusting rock that built this land could be hiding natural gas — not enough to appreciably diminish the energy problem, but perhaps enough to turn a profit on an investment. The dam sites at Sun Butte and Castle Reef will forever tempt the frustrated builders of concrete edifices. The virgin stands of timber still can be seen as board feet of lumber, as overcutting dwindles both public and private forests.

With this book begins a transition in the history of America's wilderness movement. Those who came before fought the battles for classifying major areas. Those who follow must be committed to preserving what has been painfully gained. Bulldozers, drilling rigs, chain saws and cement mixers have indeed been given pause. In reality, however, they never shut down their engines; they merely let them idle outside the boundaries.

As the mistakes of trial-and-error management, often stimulated by greed, continue to take their toll on the millions of exploitable acres, the pressures will mount. The few commodity resources protected by wilderness will tease the world's entrepreneurs like the Sirens teased Ulysses. The virgin forests of wilderness will taunt timber managers struggling with sub-par, second- and third-growth timber stands. Wilderness timber — remnants of what this nation's forests once were — will stand in silent judgment on decades of management by expediency. The firm, clear flow of water issuing from pristine watersheds will mock the depleted and silty channels already reflecting our inability to use grass, trees and land with temperance. Wilderness will be the gauge by which the future will measure the depth of the tragedy of the land and resources we once held in common. The shame of it all will raise the pitch of those screaming for access to the commodities of the last wild lands.

The wilderness can and will stand as long as the people of America demand it. This book tells of a place that will be contested as a major part of this great American drama. Learn about it and prepare to participate. The story of wild-land protection is never finished; it lives on chapter by chapter. The pen now awaits your hand. This book challenges you to pick it up.

The Bob Marshall Country

An Introduction

by Rick Graetz

With the temperature hovering at 30 degrees below zero and the snow piled high outside, the saloon in Choteau, full of warmth and holiday revelers, was most attractive. My climbing partner and I were heading toward the North Fork of the Teton Canyon for some back-country skiing and a climb of Mt. Wright. Our trek would begin about 30 miles west of town, and we were looking for a warm place to change into our winter clothing and ski boots. We were well aware that we'd be experiencing temperatures of 30 to 50 degrees below zero, and leaving the cheer of the folks dancing to western music in that bar was the hardest part of the trip. However, we were excited to meet winter head on, for we were about to face it in the epitome of wilderness, a region that has given me some of my most enjoyable wildland experiences — the Bob Marshall Country.

West of Augusta, Choteau, Bynum and Dupuyer, the Montana prairie is terminated abruptly by the spectacular towering walls of the Rocky Mountain Front. For 110 miles, this craggy limestone formation serves as the eastern rampart of the Bob Marshall Country. From Ear Mountain, a prominent Front Range peak, it is 60 miles as the eagle flies to the slopes of the equally impressive Swan Range, the Bob's western flank.

Glacier National Park and Marias Pass form the northern border, and the valley of the Blackfoot River is the southern terminus of the Bob Marshall eco-system. Its longest axis from West Glacier south to Rogers Pass is 140 miles. The area may be circled by road, a 380-mile journey, but not a single road crosses it.

This is a land of incredible diversity, a scaled down version of what the western American wilderness once was. Windswept prairie ridges, deep canyons, towering cliffs, dense forests, wild rivers, lush meadows and a diverse wildlife population — all are part of this, the crown jewel of the nation's wilderness system.

The Bob Marshall Country is big in size, grandeur and legend; it comprises the contiguous 1.5 million-acre Bob Marshall, Great Bear and Scapegoat Wilderness areas and almost one million acres of surrounding wildlands. It is home to almost every big game species found in North America, including the endangered grizzly bear. Bald and golden eagles soar from its precipitous canyon walls and even timber wolves may still roam here. The Continental Divide is its backbone.

From its interior and high country are born two of Montana's blue ribbon trout streams, the South Fork and Middle Fork of the Flathead. The South Fork gets its start on the southern boundary of the wilderness as the Danaher River, and the Middle Fork commences as a trickle via Strawberry Creek at Badger Pass along the Continental Divide.

Other major streams and rivers emanate from the divide country. They are the Sun River, draining the area on the east side of the Continental Divide; the South Fork of Two Medicine River, flowing north toward Glacier; Birch Creek, flowing east from the divide to the prairie; Badger Creek, rising from peaks of the Front Range and surging eastward; and the Dearborn River, making its headwaters along the east wall of Scapegoat Mountain and rushing southeast to the Missouri River.

This mountain country is steeped in history acted out by Indians and early-day mountain men. Its passes and river valleys served as passage ways for Indians to the west seeking the buffalo of the prairie lands beyond the mountain wall. Lewis and Clark Pass on the southern end and Gateway Pass, the headwaters area for the South Fork of Birch Creek, were favorite routes. The Blackfeet Nation controlled the lands that border the peaks on the east, and its warriors moved into the mountains to ambush tribes heading toward the plains.

Indians frequented Medicine Springs at the confluence of the North Fork and South Fork of the Sun, to the west of Gibson Lake. Pictographs are evident in this area. Atop Half Dome Crag, west of Heart Butte, native Americans received visions from the Great Spirit. The Great North Trail, used by prehistoric man and by Indian tribes in recent history, follows the Rocky Mountain Front. Travois tracks are still discernable.

Mountain ranges of this big country have a distinct northwest-southwest axis and are separated by long river valleys, some carved by glaciers.

The Rocky Mountain Front, with its great relief and towering limestone walls rising from the prairie, is the eastern-most range. It stands out as the best known of the ranges, not only because of its geographic location, but also because of controversy and popularity.

The valleys of the Two Medicine, Sun and Dearborn Rivers separate the Rocky Mountain Front from the Continental Divide Range. The dominant features of this divide chain are the Chinese Wall and Scapegoat Mountain complexes.

Spotted Bear River, the Middle Fork of the Flathead, the White River and other waterways come between the divide and a central massif of mountains. The Flathead Range to the east of Hungry Horse Lake, is the northern segment. Great Northern Mountain is the most visible summit in the area. Prominent points farther south are Silvertip Mountain and the Flathead Alps, a cluster of peaks just south of the Chinese Wall.

The big valley formed by the South Fork of the Flathead and by the Danaher divides the central range from the western-most mountains of the Swan Range. The Swan Peaks, and adjoining summits to the south and east, including those near the town of Lincoln, Montana and the Monture Creek country, represent the largest of the mountain masses of the Bob Marshall Country.

Compared to other Montana mountains, the peaks of the Bob Marshall are not high. None top 10,000 feet. Red Mountain, 9,411 feet, is the highest. However, it is relief that counts, and these mountains look higher than many others. Heavy snow loads, especially on the Swan Range and the peaks just south of Glacier Park have helped maintain a few high cirque glaciers. These small alpine ice fields, existing on the slopes of Swan Peak, Holland Peak and Great Northern Mountain, are remnants of the big valley glaciers that helped sculpture the wilderness.

This pristine country is known for its mixture of big meadows and dense forest cover. Coniferous trees, including ponderosa pine, larch, Douglas fir and lodgepole pine, abound as do aspen and cottonwood. The wildlands of the Bob Marshall, Scapegoat and Great Bear offer abundant wildflowers and beargrass. The meadows along the east side of the Chinese Wall and Scapegoat Mountain present some of the most beautiful displays of beargrass in Montana.

Virtually all the terrain of the wilderness country and surrounding land is under U.S. Forest Service control and is accessible to the public. The sharp rise of the Swan Range and an absence of numerous canyons limit access on the west, but all other areas are reached easily by roads to or near the wilderness boundary. The Rocky Mountain Front on the east and the southern areas have more entry points. Horseback riding is a popular way to visit the back country and many outfitters and guides offer trips for sightseeing, hunting, fishing and floating. Backpacking, snowshoeing and skiing are probably the most intimate ways to explore this big land. An excellent trail system provides routes in all directions. The roads that lead into or near the wilderness boundary provide a great sampling of what is available in the back country. Forest Service campgrounds along these routes are for the enjoyment of those not able to, or not desiring to, hike the land beyond.

The Bob may be visited any time of the year, but it is easiest to travel the back country in the summer months. Spring, with its melting snows and high run-offs, is perhaps the least desirable time. Peak run-off can occur between early May and mid-June. By mid-June most of the smaller streams can be crossed. The bigger waterways are still running fast and deep until about the second week in July.

The heaviest human use is from early July until early September. Later in September and on into late November come the hunters. Travel, especially beyond the trails, without skis or snowshoes, becomes difficult after mid-November, and sometimes much sooner.

The Bob Marshall Country offers a myriad of wilderness experiences. For me it has created a priceless collection of memories ... standing atop the Chinese Wall with a fresh wind blowing in my face as air was lifted from the west ... a full moon illuminating snow covered Silvertip Mountain ... storm clouds lifting to unveil the sheer face of the Swan Range ... peaceful walks through Big River Meadows ... watching hundreds of elk graze on the slopes above the North Fork of the Sun ... skiing untracked deep powder near Circle Creek ... picking wild strawberries along the South Fork of Birch Creek ... fly fishing the wild South Fork of the Flathead ... watching lightning bolts strike the rocks around me on top of Scapegoat Mountain ... virtually swimming in a sea of beargrass along Halfmoon Creek ... standing on the summit of Mount Wright at 40 below zero viewing countless rainbows floating in the ice-crystal-filled air of the valleys below ... gazing in awe at the incredible expanse of wild country stretched out before me from the top of Rocky Mountain Peak.

This untamed land is many things to many people. Most of all it is a chance to experience wilderness at its best. One visit will convince almost anyone that wilderness is worth saving. The Bob Marshall Country is indeed a national treasure. Thanks to the foresight of early-day conservationists, these mountains, canyons, rivers and valleys will remain wild and free.

In recent years Montana sportsmen have established three Rocky Mountain Front wildlife preserves, the Sun River, Ear Mountain and Blackleaf game ranges, to protect the wildlife population. Other private efforts, namely through the work of the Nature Conservancy, have resulted in the creation of the Pine Butte Swamp Preserve. Today, because of their concern, the elk and deer population of the Rocky Mountain Front area is far greater than at the turn of the century, and the big horn sheep herd that roams this area is one of the largest and most important in the nation.

Recent petitions to the Forest Service by energy companies for rights to explore for oil and gas ran into tremendous public opposition. People who may never see the back country of the Bob Marshall rallied to the cry "Save the Bob." Why? To them, as well as to those who have visited it, the Bob Marshall country is the "type specimen," the artist's first wax. It is the essence of wilderness, and they are happy to know such a place exists.

— — — — — — —

What follows is an attempt to portray the Bob Marshall Country by way of text and photography. I have asked others with a special knowledge of certain subjects to contribute their work, and I believe their various writing styles add to the interest of the book. We will look first at the geology, weather, wildlife and history of the Bob Marshall Country, and then divide this vast land into geographic regions to get a feeling for the special qualities of each. The text and the photographs will be easier to follow with a map for reference. The Lewis and Clark National Forest (Rocky Mountain Division) and Flathead National Forest (South Half) maps will suffice as they show all the country featured here. Elsewhere you'll find addresses to write for maps.

Although trails and access are discussed, they are not covered in depth; maps show all this. It is my hope that this book will give you the insight to pick your own routes of travel and to challenge you to find your favorite spot in the "Bob."

CHAPTER ONE

Geology

The Overthrust Belt

by Dave Alt

In one form and another, the overthrust belt winds a varied and more or less disconnected course from the arctic end of the Canadian Rockies to Central America. But the province is not nearly as simple as a long, curving line on a map might suggest. Geologists who try to trace the overthrust belt find that its different segments consist of quite different rock formations; and it is difficult to find several geologists who can easily agree on exactly how one segment connects with the next.

However, all portions of the overthrust belt do resemble each other in consisting of rock formations that slid generally eastward, perhaps 50 miles or more, during formation of the Rocky Mountains. That happened slowly, probably during a period of several million years, and it did not happen at the same time in all parts of the overthrust belt. In round numbers, we can say that it happened about 70 million years ago, give or take 10 million or so years. That was about the time that the dinosaurs reached the peak of their development, and then abruptly vanished — there is no reason to suppose that the two events were in any way related.

Now the displaced rocks of the overthrust belt exist in complexly jumbled structures in which older formations tend to lie on top of younger ones, exactly the reverse of their normal order. That arrangement formed through generally eastward sliding during development of the Rocky Mountains unites the various segments of the overthrust belt into a loosely continuous geologic province. Let us look more closely at one segment of that province, the northern Montana portion of the overthrust belt.

Considered from a geologic point of view, that portion of the overthrust belt is really a southern extension of the Canadian Rockies. Rocks do not respect political boundaries. The northern Montana portion of the overthrust belt consists of the mountains of Glacier Park, and of the Sawtooth Range, which extends from Glacier Park almost to Helena and includes the Bob Marshall and Scapegoat Wilderness areas. All those mountains share the same general geologic history, which begins more than a billion years ago with deposition of the oldest sedimentary formations.

9

The Beginning of the Story

A billion or so years ago, during that remote period geologists call the Precambrian Era, the western margin of our continent was about where the western border of Idaho is today. There were no animals yet, and the highest forms of life were primitive blue-green algae similar to some of those that still form scummy growths in quiet pools of water. Thick sequences of layered sediments destined to become formations of mudstone, sandstone, and limestone were accumulating, some in shallow water, others on more or less dry land. Those rocks now form a large and conspicuous part of the northern Montana overthrust belt, virtually all of Glacier Park, and most of the western part of the Sawtooth Range. No one knows how thick the section of Precambrian sedimentary rocks is, but it amounts to some tens of thousands of feet — an enormously thick pile.

Anyone, geologist or not, can rather easily learn to recognize those Precambrian sedimentary rocks. They consist mostly of colorful red and green mudstones, limestones in many shades of gray, and sandstones in a wide spectrum of colors ranging from white through yellow to red. Streams round fragments of those rocks into pebbles that make brightly colorful deposits of gravel, beautiful beds for sparkling mountain streams. People who look closely at individual pebbles, or at the bedrock outcrops from which they came, find an abundance of exquisitely preserved sedimentary structures.

Paper-thin sedimentary layers make patterns of fine stripes in many pebbles. The same layers appear in many bedrock outcrops along with perfectly recognizable sand ripples, layers of suncracked mud, raindrop imprints, and many other structures. They tell us something about the world of a billion years ago: that waves and running water ruffled soft sand or mud into ripples then just as they do now, and that the sun sometimes baked drying mud into intricate patterns of cracks just like those we see in roadside puddles today. Sometimes a passing shower left those mud surfaces imprinted with little dents recording a sprinkle of raindrops. How could such delicate features survive so long?

Many younger sedimentary rocks contain similar structures, but rarely so perfectly preserved, or in such spectacular abundance. The difference seems to lie in the absence of animals from the Precambrian scene. Nothing rooted around in those layers of soft mud and sand as they accumulated, so the original sedimentary features remained undisturbed as they were buried and the soft sediments eventually hardened into solid rock.

It is possible to find abundant fossil remains of blue-green algae in many of the Precambrian sedimentary rocks. They appear in a variety of forms, most commonly as inconspicuous and paper-thin laminations in the rock. Those were simply scummy growths of algae that covered the mud surface and were then buried beneath another accumulation of mud. Here and there, in places where growing conditions were most favorable, the algae developed structures called stromatolites, which look at first glance as though they might be fossil cabbages, although stromatolites and cabbages are related only in that both are plants. Stromatolites may be as small as brussels sprouts, or as large as washtubs, and in many places they form massive reefs. The fossil blue-green algae deserve a certain degree of respect from all of us because they were the first green plants. They started the long process of transforming the earth's early atmosphere into a breathable composition. That made it possible for animals to appear on our planet; and that event ended the Precambrian Era.

The first animals appeared, abruptly and in some considerable variety, about 570 million years ago. That was the beginning of the Cambrian Period, and also of the Paleozoic Era, which includes six more geologic periods. Animals evolve continuously, so the changing fashions of their fossil remains subdivide the time since they appeared into a series of geologic periods.

The last of the Precambrian sedimentary rocks seems to have formed sometime before the first animals appeared, perhaps as much as few hundred million years before. Sometime around the middle of Cambrian Time, about 550 million years ago, our region sank slightly below sea level. Cambrian sedimentary rocks, some of them full of animal fossils, accumulated to a total thickness between 1,000 and 2,000 feet. That is only a small fraction of the amount of Precambrian sedimentary rock. Nevertheless, the Cambrian rocks are conspicuous in some parts of the Sawtooth Range because they include massive beds of limestone that make bold cliffs and high ridges. The Chinese Wall, one of the best-known landmarks in the Bob Marshall Wilderness, is a high cliff carved in Cambrian limestone.

The fossils tell us that there is a gap after Cambrian Time, that the next sedimentary rocks began to accumulate during Devonian Time, about 390 million years ago. Layers of sedimentary rock then continued to accumulate, with no extremely long interruptions until the end of the Paleozoic Era, approximately 225 million years ago. Between 5,000 and 6,000 feet of Paleozoic sedimentary rock accumulated after Cambrian Time, and geologists divide it into about a dozen formations. Some of those formations are conspicuous in the landscape of the Sawtooth Range.

It is virtually impossible to visit the eastern part of the Sawtooth Range without noticing the Madison Limestone. It is about 2,000 feet thick in most areas, and always seems to form awesome cliffs and ridges, including the high ridge that forms the eastern rampart of the range. A close look at outcrops of the Madison Limestone often reveals fossil corals, some of which look almost like honeycombs embedded in the rock. The Jefferson Dolomite is another ridge- and cliff-forming body of rock. It is generally dark brown or black, and it stinks when freshly broken. Both the dark color and the foul smell are caused by abundant organic matter trapped in the rock.

The Mesozoic Era began about 225 million years ago as the Paleozoic Era ended, and it lasted until about 65 million years ago. This was the time when the dinosaurs roamed the earth, and their sudden disappearance defines the end of the era. The Mesozoic Era was also a time when more formations of layered sedimentary rocks, about 1,500 feet of them, accumulated in our region. None of those rock units makes high ridges; they tend instead to contribute to the landscape by eroding into deep valleys.

Toward the end of Mesozoic Time, when the last of the sedimentary formations were accumulating, volcanoes were erupting in the area between Helena and Butte. Large masses of molten granite magma were rising into the upper part of the earth's crust in that area, and some of it erupted to make a thick pile of volcanic rocks, and to fill the air with clouds of volcanic ash. Much of that volcanic pile has since eroded away to reveal the granite that crystallized beneath it, but enough remains to tell the story. Some of the volcanic ash survives in the late Mesozoic sedimentary rocks in the Sawtooth Range, and along the east side of Glacier Park. We find it in somber greenish sandstones, and in occasional beds of bentonite clay, which is an altered form of volcanic ash.

None of the older sedimentary formations contains volcanic ash. Its appearance in the late Mesozoic rocks signals the beginning of crustal movements that would soon transform our region from a broad plain near sea level to ranges of high mountains. Events in the Northern Rocky Mountains were actually a small part of a much larger pattern that affected much of the earth.

From Plains to Overthrust Belt

As the Mesozoic Era began, the American continents were joined to Europe and Africa to make an enormous supercontinent that included most the earth's land area. The Atlantic Ocean did not exist then, and the Pacific Ocean was much broader than it now is. Then, about 200 million years ago, that supercontinent split, and pieces began to move apart as the Atlantic Ocean opened between them. That movement still continues, and still causes major geologic activity in many parts of the world. Formation of the Rocky Mountains was one of its earlier consequences.

Something must give if a continent starts moving across the face of the earth. In this case, the floor of the Pacific Ocean buckled and began to slide beneath the western margins of the American continents, and then down into the earth's interior. Meanwhile, new oceanic crust formed in the middle of the Atlantic Ocean as it grew wider. The disappearing floor of the Pacific Ocean was primarily responsible for the creation of the Rocky Mountains, and of the overthrust belt.

As the sinking oceanic crust reached a depth of about 60 miles, its upper part melted and rose toward the surface. By late Mesozoic time, that was happening on a large scale in the western part of our region, and enormous masses of granite magma were rising into the upper part of the continent in the area that is now central and northern Idaho and westernmost Montana. Emplacement of those enormous masses of granite, one after the

11

a

b

(a) Below Cliff Mountain on the southern end of the Chinese Wall looking toward the Flathead Alps. An excellent example of the sheer east-facing cliffs and the more gently sloping western side of the mountains typical of the overthrust belt in this area. U.S. Forest Service photo. (b) Part of the Rocky Mountain Front Range looking at Our Lake. U.S. Forest Service photo. (c) Above Deep Creek looking south along the Rocky Mountain Front. Castle Reef is the formation in the middle of the photo. Overthrust geology at its best. U.S. Forest Service photo. (d) Peaks of the Rocky Mountain Front looking north up Blacktail Gulch. U.S. Forest Service photo.

c

d

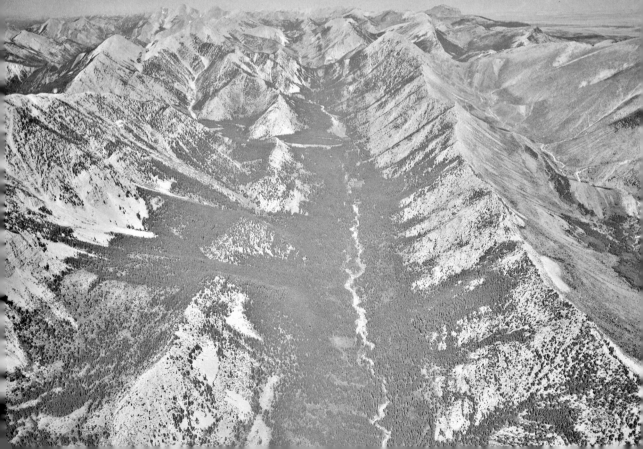

other over a period of millions of years, bulged the earth's surface up as though there were an enormous blister beneath. The bulge must have been at least several thousand feet high, and it covered most of central and northern Idaho as well as the western fringes of Montana. It contributed to formation of the overthrust belt by raising and tilting all those thousands of feet of layered sedimentary rocks that had been accumulating in our region since Precambrian Time.

We think of rocks as rigid and unyielding because they seem that way in our everyday experience. But ours is a limited and rather unrevealing view. On the scale of the earth's crust, and in the endless expanses of geologic time, rocks behave as though they had almost no strength, almost as though they were so much warm gelatin. It is impossible to raise and tilt a thick accumulation of sedimentary layers of regional extent without causing them to move.

Compare the situation of the sedimentary section in the northern Rockies at the end of Mesozoic Time to that of a thick stack of heavily buttered pancakes on a tilted platter. That is a perilously unstable situation. We could expect the stronger rocks, such as limestone or sandstone, to behave in a manner comparable to the pancakes while the weaker rocks, such as shale, lubricated the stack as though they were so much melted butter. The entire section of layered sedimentary rocks responded to the tilting by doing about what we would expect of the pancakes. It slid. The layers of rock moved generally eastward, because that was the downhill direction, and piled up in great slabs to form the complexly jumbled structures that comprise the overthrust belt.

Several kinds of evidence provide clues to when that all happened. We know that the overthrust belt could not have begun to form much before the end of the Mesozoic Era because very late Mesozoic sedimentary rocks were involved. On the other hand, the earliest rocks deposited during the succeeding Cenozoic Era are not deformed, so movement must have been complete before those sediments accumulated. The time window between those limits reaches from about 75 to about 55 million years ago, in round numbers. Other, more subtle clues lead most geologists to believe that overthrust belt deformation must have happened during the earlier part of that period, perhaps about 70 million years ago.

We have no way of knowing exactly how far the slabs of rock in the overthrust belt moved. However, it seems quite likely that many of the rocks in the northern Montana overthrust belt must have travelled at least 50 miles to reach their present positions. Some may have moved even farther. In other words, many of the rocks we see today in the Sawtooth Range and in Glacier Park must have accumulated as sediments in northwestern Montana, or possibly even in northern Idaho. The rocks now at the surface in those regions formed at some considerable depths, so it is perfectly conceivable that they are exposed now because the rocks that formerly covered them moved off and into the overthrust belt.

Neither is it possible to know exactly how long it took the rocks in the overthrust belt to move into their present positions. But we can be sure that there is no reason to suppose they moved rapidly. Most geologists assume that the rocks moved very slowly, probably during a period of at least several million years. For example, if the rocks moved at a rate of one inch per year, they could travel 50 miles within about 3 million years. That is the sort of thing most geologists envision, even though they have no solid information on the actual rate of movement.

Overthrust Faulting

Visitors to the Sawtooth Range notice almost immediately that the landscape is built on a basic framework of high ridges and deep valleys that continue for many miles, and trend generally from north to south. Many of those ridges and valleys are remarkably straight. That distinctive landscape vividly expresses the geologic structure of the overthrust belt.

Each long ridge is the outcrop of a resistant layer of rock, each valley the exposure of a layer that erodes easily. The ridges stand high because erosion removed the less resistant rock to carve deep valleys. The long ridges and valleys trend from north to south because the layers of sedimentary rock trend that way.

A quick look at the landscape, and at the rocks themselves, shows that the Sawtooth Range consists basically of sedimentary rocks tilted gently down to the west. The upturned edges of the layers trend from north to south simply because that direction is at right angles to the way they tilt. Look at the shingles on a roof, and see that their edges trend at right angles to the direction the roof slopes.

Landscapes consisting of fairly straight and parallel ridges and valleys are fairly common. In most cases, they form where erosion has carved out the less resistant layers in a folded or tilted sequence of sedimentary rocks, leaving the more resistant layers to stand high as long ridges. However, anyone who learns to recognize even a few of the different rock formations in the Sawtooth Range quickly discovers that the situation there is far more complex than simple folding or tilting. Consider, for example, the sequence of rock formations along the road through the Sun River Canyon west of Augusta, the place where many visitors first enter the Sawtooth Range.

Castle Reef, the high ridge that forms the abrupt eastern front of the Sawtooth Range in the Sun River area, is an enormous slab of Madison Limestone tilted gently down to the west. Several formations that normally lie on top of the Madison Limestone are exposed in the valley west of that ridge, exactly as one would expect. Then things get more complicated. The next ridge west of that valley is another slab of Madison Limestone, also tilted down to the west. That is absolutely astonishing because the second slab of Madison Limestone must lie on top of rock formations younger than itself, the reverse of the normal and proper order. Then the situation repeats itself again with another valley followed by still another high ridge of Madison Limestone. The pattern continues beyond the end of the road and westward through the range, except that the rock formations involved become progressively older westward. There is a succession of ridges composed of the Jefferson Formation, then of the Cambrian Limestones, and finally of various Precambrian formations.

There is only one way to get a big slab of Madison Limestone, or any other formation, on top of rocks younger than itself, and that is by faulting. Those big slabs of rock must have slid over the younger rocks along a surface that slopes gently down to the west. Geologists call such surfaces of slippage overthrust faults. The Sawtooth Range contains numerous overthrust faults, more than a dozen large ones and many more lesser ones. The range consists of a series of large slabs of rock that slid eastward into their present positions along those faults. Each successive overthrust slab lies on top of and overlaps its neighbor to the east like so many shingles on a roof.

Geologists have long wondered how large slabs of rock can move on such gently sloping fault surfaces. And the curious overlapping pattern of overthrust slabs in the Sawtooth Range with the rocks becoming progressively older from east to west presents another problem.

Even now, almost a century after the phenomenon was first recognized, geologists have trouble understanding overthrust faulting. How does a sheet of rock thousands of feet thick that extends over hundreds or even thousands of square miles slide almost horizontally for long distances?

For many years, geologists assumed that something must push those slabs from behind. Unfortunately for that idea, there is nothing behind most of those slabs that could possibly have pushed them. The Swan and Mission Valleys lie west of the Sawtooth Range, and neither could have given much of a shove. Furthermore, it is easy to show that a force applied from behind would crumple those overthrust slabs into folds long before it could overcome the frictional resistance to their movement. After all, a slab a few thousand feet thick that extends over hundreds or perhaps thousands of square miles has dimensions resembling those of a carpet, so the problem is a bit like getting behind a large carpet and then trying to shove it unrumpled across a rough floor.

The problem becomes much simpler if we think of overthrust slabs moving downhill under the pull of gravity, instead of in response to a push from behind. Gravity exerts its force equally on every particle of rock in the slab, so there is no need to think of a force pushing from behind. However, that leaves unanswered the question of how an overthrust slab can move despite the enormous friction along the fault surface.

Some geologists argue that overthrust slabs could move almost without friction if the pore spaces in the rocks contain water under extremely high pressure. Under those conditions, the water would help support the weight of the overthrust slab. That would greatly reduce friction along the fault surface and thus lubricate movement of the slab. However, many of the rocks in the overthrust belt contain very little pore space, and that makes it difficult to imagine that water could have played an important role in their movement.

Most geologists now suspect that overthrust fault movement probably involves slippage on the weaker beds of rock. The thick layers of relatively strong rock such as limestone and sandstone seem to slide on beds of shale or mudstone as though they were on grease. Water in the pores of the rocks probably does help in some cases, although certainly not in all. In

15

any case, it is clear that overthrust slabs must move with virtually no friction along the fault surface because they glide down extremely gentle slopes, and the rock near the fault surface shows little evidence of breakage.

The arrangement of overthrust slabs in the Sawtooth Range with older rocks tending to overlap younger ones from east to west presents another problem. Geologists have proposed a number of theories to explain that arrangement, so far without coming to anything resembling general agreement. One of the simpler theories proposes that the overthrust slabs peeled off the uplifted pile of sedimentary rocks in sequence from the top down. The first slab to move consisted of the youngest rocks from the top of the pile, then a second slab consisting of older rocks followed, and so on down the sequence. The first slab now forms the eastern margin of the range with those that followed piled on each other in succession from east to west. That scenario explains some, but not all, of the strange arrangement we see in the Sawtooth Range — none of the theories so far proposed seems to explain everything.

Although Glacier Park is part of the northern Montana overthrust belt, the structure and the landscape there differ considerably from what we see in the Sawtooth Range. Most of Glacier Park consists of a single enormous overthrust slab composed entirely of Precambrian sedimentary rocks that slid east on the Lewis overthrust fault. We can see the fault surface exposed for many miles along the eastern and southern margins of the park where it separates Precambrian rocks above from much younger late Mesozoic sedimentary rocks below. An abrupt break in slope marks the fault because the resistant Precambrian rocks above it erode very slowly to make steep cliffs, whereas the late Mesozoic rocks beneath erode more easily into gently rolling topography. Glacier Park lacks the regular succession of parallel ridges and valleys we see in the Sawtooth Range because it consists of a single overthrust slab that lies almost horizontally, instead of a series of them stacked on each other like shingles on a roof.

Oil and Gas

The first oil wells in Montana were drilled shortly after the turn of the century in an area since flooded by Sherburne Reservoir just below the Many Glacier Hotel in Glacier Park. They produced minuscule amounts of oil from late Mesozoic sedimentary rocks at depths of less than 200 feet. That oil field never did amount to much, and it was abandoned after a few months of hectic activity. Geologists considered it a freak.

For many years, most geologists doubted that any part of the overthrust belt would produce much oil or gas. They believed that the rocks are so broken that most of any petroleum they might have contained must have leaked out leaving amounts too small to be commercially worthwhile. Furthermore, the intense deformation of the rocks in all parts of the province made it seem likely that any oil and gas fields that might exist would be small and exceedingly difficult to find. Those opinions changed during the late 1970s with significant petroleum discoveries in the Alberta and Wyoming portions of the overthrust belt. Now there is intense interest in the northern Montana portion.

There is no reason to doubt that geologic structures similar to those that trapped natural gas in the Alberta portion of the overthrust belt probably exist beneath Glacier Park and the Sawtooth Range. But those traps may or may not contain petroleum.

Remember that our region was a vast plain underlain by thick sequences of sedimentary rocks until the Rocky Mountains formed about 70 million years ago. Then the layers of rock underlying the western part of that plain broke up and slid eastward over the plains to make the overthrust belt. Meanwhile, the same formations east of the mountain front remained almost undisturbed. The rocks you see while hiking the ridges in the Sawtooth Range belong to the same formations that lie beneath the plains to the east.

Oil exploration people envision two general targets in the overthrust belt: the big slabs of rock that slid eastward during formation of the Rocky Mountains, and the less disturbed rocks belonging to the same formations that lie buried beneath the overthrust slabs. It should be perfectly possible to drill a deep well almost anywhere in the overthrust belt and penetrate the same formations twice: first in the overthrust slabs, and then again at depth beneath them. Both of those targets involve the same rock formations that lie beneath the plains immediately east of the overthrust belt.

In both Alberta and Wyoming, the plains east of the overthrust belt contain numerous oil and gas fields. They provide excellent direct evidence that the formations in the overthrust

Preceding page, top: *Sawtooth Ridge on the Rocky Mountain Front and the Sun River game range west of Augusta, Rick Graetz;* **bottom:** *the Rocky Mountain Front, Castle Reef on the left, Rick Graetz.*

This page, top: *Swift Reservoir in early fall, Rick Graetz;* **bottom:** *the Rocky Mountain Front in winter looking toward the Sun River country, Gus Wolfe.*
Opposite page, top: *Big George Gulch from above Gibson Lake, Rick Graetz;* **bottom:** *the Rocky Mountain Front from the Benchmark Road looking toward Sawtooth Mountain on the left and Haystack Butte on the right. Rick Graetz*

Top: *fall in Hannan Gulch. Bill Lancaster*
Bottom: *looking down Willow Creek toward the prairie. Gus Wolfe*

Top: *looking down Mortimer Gulch toward Gibson Lake. Rick Graetz*
Bottom: *Home Gulch and Sawtooth. Bill Lancaster*

*This page, top: from above Mortimer Gulch looking toward Prairie Reef and the Slategoat Mountain area, Rick Graetz; **bottom:** looking up Hannan Gulch with Castle Reef on the right, Bill Lancaster*
Opposite page, top: *fall on the Rocky Mountain Front looking toward Castle Reef, Bill Lancaster; **bottom:** Castle Reef and Hannan Gulch from the air, Rick Graetz*

Choteau Mountain along the Rocky Mountain Front. Rocky Mountain Peak is the highest peak on the left and Old Baldy is the highest point on the right horizon. Rick Graetz

Top: *from above Mortimer Gulch, looking toward Mortimer Peak on the left. Rick Graetz*
Bottom: *fall on the Rocky Mountain Front west of Augusta. Gus Wolfe*

Top: *Blackleaf Canyon in the winter. U.S. Forest Service Photo — J.F. Higgins*
Bottom: *fall on the Rocky Mountain Front west of Augusta. Gus Wolfe*

Top: *looking down Home Gulch from the west slopes of Sawtooth Ridge. Rick Graetz*
Bottom left: *the Sun River below Gibson Lake. Rick Graetz*
Bottom right: *Tom Brokaw fishing the North Fork of the Sun River. Rick Graetz*

Top: Ear Mountain on the Rocky Mountain Front west of Choteau. Rick Graetz
Center: the Rocky Mountain Front and the Dearborn Canyon area. Rick Graetz
Below: from the top of Arsenic Peak, looking over the North Fork of the Sun River country. Rick Graetz

Opposite page, top: Bill Cunningham, Jay Hutchinson, and Ellie Arguimbau atop Prairie Reef looking toward the North Fork of the Sun River country and the Rocky Mountain Front ranges, Rick Graetz; bottom: above the North Fork of the Sun in winter looking toward Slategoat Mountain, Rick Graetz

This page, top: Yvon Chouinard and Rick Ridgeway fishing the North Fork of the Sun River, Rick Graetz; bottom: Gates Park Ranger Station in the North Fork of the Sun River country, Rick Graetz

Top: *Barbara Bennetts skiing the valley of the North Fork of the Sun River. Rick Graetz*
Bottom: *Ray Mills with pack string heading up the west side of Headquarters Pass. U.S. Forest Service Photo — R.M. Richmond*

belt contain petroleum. It is therefore no great surprise to see successful wildcat wells in the Alberta and Wyoming portions of the overthrust belt. In Montana, on the other hand, more than 30 years of fairly determined exploration drilling in the plains east of the Sawtooth Range has so far produced very little indication of petroleum beyond some natural gas in the area west of Augusta. There is therefore little apparent reason to assume that drilling in the same formations in the Sawtooth Range will be any more successful. Nevertheless, interest in the area remains high.

The first step in petroleum exploration is seismic profiling. That involves detonating charges of dynamite and then recording the echoes reflected from layers of rock at depth. Interpretation of those echoes from a large number of such charges reveals the pattern in which the rock layers are folded and faulted, places where oil and natural gas would accumulate if any were present in the formation. However, seismic profiles do not reveal whether petroleum exists at depth, only where it would be trapped if it does exist. The only way to determine whether potential oil and gas traps actually contain anything is by drilling. There is no alternative, no other way to finally determine whether petroleum reserves exist.

Exploration drilling is rarely a simple matter that leads quickly to a conclusion. Consider for example the history of the Wyoming portion of the overthrust belt where exploration drilling began in 1868, in an area where oil was actually seeping to the surface. After that, at least 141 wells were drilled to make two significant discoveries, one in 1925 and the next in 1976. It is certainly true that exploration methods are more efficient now than in the past, and that makes it possible to evaluate a province in less time, and with fewer wells. Even so, evaluation of the oil and gas prospects in the Sawtooth Range would inevitably be a long process involving many wells drilled over a period of many years.

That prospect becomes alarming when we consider that much of the Sawtooth Range is in the Bob Marshall and Scapegoat Wilderness Areas, and that Glacier Park is also in the northern Montana portion of the overthrust belt. Petroleum exploration in those areas would entail the inevitable sacrifice of known and well established wilderness values in exchange for entirely conjectural oil and gas reserves that might or might not be found at some unknown future time. Furthermore, there is now no sound reason to assume that those reserves exist, nor will there be until a number of large discoveries are made in the plains east of the Sawtooth Range.

Even the most optimistic estimates of the hypothetical petroleum reserves in the northern Montana portion of the overthrust belt are modest. No one suggests that the province could become a major source of petroleum, no one supposes that it could satisfy the national appetite for more than a few weeks, at most.

The Landscape

Mountain building ceased in the northern Montana portion of the overthrust belt some tens of millions of years ago, and has little direct influence on the details of the modern landscape. The hills and valleys we see there today owe their origin almost entirely to erosion, especially to erosion during the last several million years ago. Let us begin by going back to the Pliocene Epoch, which ended about 2 or 3 million years ago, and then follow the development of the landscape to the present.

During Pliocene Time, our region was extremely arid, a desert probably comparable to that in the Death Valley area today. In such regions, streams flow into the valleys where they disappear as the water sinks into the ground, and evaporates. No water and no sediment leave such regions, so the valleys fill with deposits of mud, sand and gravel as the mountains erode away. As time passes, the mountains slowly drown in their own debris.

Meanwhile, more sediment spread eastward from the mountain front in a vast apron that sloped very gently down to the east. Except in its enormous scale, it resembled the aprons of sediment that spread from the base of an eroding roadcut, or pile of fill dirt. By the end of Pliocene Time, the mountains of the Sawtooth Range and Glacier National Park must have presented a subdued and uninspiring spectacle, low peaks rising at the head of a vast and nearly featureless plain that sloped gently away to the east and to the west from the crest of the range. That bleak and arid scene set the stage for development of the modern landscape.

Pliocene Time ended, and the Pleistocene Epoch began, sometime between 2 and 3 million years ago. And it was about then that the first of the great ice ages spread enormous glaciers over much of the northern hemisphere. At about the same time, the climate became much wetter, wet enough that permanent streams began to flow, to join together to form larger streams, and to drain the region to the ocean. Those streams that began to flow then survive as our modern streams, and the authors of our modern landscape.

Our modern streams began to flow on a plains surface above the level of most of the higher ridges in the modern landscape. Only a few high peaks rose above the plain then. Of course they flowed downhill, to the east or to the west according to the way that ancient plain sloped, and the divide established then survives as the continental divide.

The new streams began the long job of excavating all the sediment that had accumulated when the region was a desert, and hauling it off to the ocean. They have accomplished quite a bit during the past 2 or 3 million years, but the job is far from finished, and enough of that sediment remains to tell the story. And as they eroded their courses deeper, the streams began to bite into bedrock.

By the time those streams encountered bedrock, they were well entrenched in their channels. That gave them no choice. They could not leave those established channels to find an easier course across less resistant bedrock because that would require them to flow uphill, an impossibility. Instead, they had to carve their courses down through the resistant bedrock regardless of how hard it might be. Meanwhile, tributary drainages developed from the primary streams.

In the Sawtooth Range, those secondary drainages followed the less resistant layers of rock to erode those long, north-to-south trending valleys that so vividly express the geologic structure of the range. As the streams eroded those long valleys deeper, the resistant ridges between them stood in increasingly greater relief; erosion has been etching out the softer parts of that landscape while leaving the harder parts relatively untouched. During the last 2 to 3 million years that have passed since the climate changed at the end of Pliocene Time, erosion has greatly increased the topographic relief in the Sawtooth Range — we tend to assume that erosion softens a landscape, but that is not always true.

We can easily recognize the primary streams in the Sawtooth Range because they cut right across the grain of the landscape. The Sun River and Birch Creek are excellent examples. They, and the other streams that cut right through the high ridges, were superimposed on the modern landscape from that old desert surface that existed at the end of Pliocene Time. They began to flow in their present courses before erosion of the tributary valleys etched those ridges out of the landscape. The depth of the gorges in which they pass through the high ridges expresses the effect of something between 2 and 3 million years of erosion. And the difference in elevation between valley floor and ridge crest will continue to increase as erosion continues to reduce the general level of the landscape.

The landscape developed a bit differently in Glacier Park because the geologic structure of the rocks at the surface is simpler there. Most of the park consists of a single big overthrust slab of Precambrian sedimentary rock in which the layers have very little tilt. There are no layers of less resistant rock, which streams could preferentially erode, no way that erosion could etch out a topographic expression of the bedrock structure. So the landscape in Glacier Park is a fairly random array of ridges and valleys that lacks the pronounced topographic grain we see in the Sawtooth Range.

Of course, the last 2 or 3 million years have also been a time of many great ice ages, no one knows how many, perhaps as many as 20. They left their mark on the landscape of the Sawtooth Range and of Glacier Park.

So far as we know, glaciers do not create new valleys where none existed before. Instead, they fill existing valleys with rivers of ice that scour them out, and leave them beautifully transformed, without significantly changing the basic pattern of the drainage.

The ice-age glaciers seem to have spawned high on the mountain slopes, in places where winter snowfall exceeded summer snowmelt. Under those conditions, ice accumulates from year to year until the mass finally becomes thick enough to flow under its own weight — a thickness something more than about 150 feet. When the ice begins to flow, it ceases to be a permanent snowfield, and becomes a glacier in the proper sense of the word. Glaciers flow down their valleys, impelled by the weight of new ice forming at their heads, until they finally descend to an elevation where the climate is warm enough to melt the ice as fast as it advances.

In Glacier Park and in much of the Sawtooth Range, ice accumulated in the high mountains, and then flowed down the tributary valleys and into the main valleys to form enormous glaciers. When ice-age glaciation was at a maximum, the landscape must have consisted essentially of ridges and high peaks rising like peninsulas and islands of rock above a sea of groaning ice. Some of the big glaciers flowed out of the mountains and onto the plains where they spread out to make enormous ponds of ice along the range front.

The last ice age ended about 10,000 years ago in round numbers, an extremely short time ago by geologic reckoning. All available evidence indicates that the last ice age ended quite suddenly, so we must assume that the climate changed rather rapidly. We do not know exactly what happened, why the ice age ended, or for that matter why it began. But we can see its record in the landscape.

The most obvious signs of mountain glaciation are high on the mountain slopes where the glaciers formed. The upper part of a valley glacier is a powerful quarrying machine because the ice freezes fast to its bedrock floor, and then pulls chunks of rock free and carries them away as it flows downslope. After the ice-age glaciers melted, they left deep hollows called cirques scooped in the high mountain slopes where the head of the glacier quarried the bedrock. Cirques may be as much as several miles across, although most are somewhat less than a mile across, and many contain one or more little lakes in their floors. Nothing in the mountains is much prettier than the great cliff headwall of a cirque, hundreds of feet high, mirrored in a little lake in the floor of the hollow. That view is always worth a hike.

In many places, two or more glaciers formed high on the slopes of the same mountain, each creating its own cirque. Now that the ice has melted, those mountains rise as craggy pinnacles, called horn peaks, that drop away into deep cirque hollows. Those sharp and ragged mountain peaks are the most frequent kind of glacial sculpture, a signature of the ice age.

Below the cirque, glaciated valleys generally descend as rather steep walled troughs, many of which contain a chain of little rock basin lakes, called tarns, in their floors. A sparkling stream cascades from one charming little lake to another along the floors of those valleys, and the tributary streams enter by way of cascades, or waterfalls. Mountain glaciation is the only geologic process that can create such a valley.

Valley glaciers also tend to straighten their courses, presumably because ice goes around bends less easily than water. Now that the ice-age glaciers have melted, the valleys they once filled are left much straighter than they would have been had streams alone carved them. We all appreciate that, usually without giving it much thought, when we stand at the lower end of a long valley and see distant craggy peaks framed in its sides. Those are the views that landscape photographers and painters can never resist, and they would not exist had it not been for the ice-age glaciers.

The lower parts of glaciated valleys tend to have broad floors deeply underlain by deposits of sediment left there as the ice melted. Lakes, ponds and marshes abound, all flooding depressions in the sediment surface, and the stream tends to wander aimlessly among them. Most of the watery depressions probably mark places where masses of stagnant ice were left stranded as the glacier melted and then were buried in the deposits of sediment and finally melted. That kind of valley floor is also characteristic of glaciated mountains, although it is the product of glacial deposition rather than glacial sculpture.

The glaciers are gone now, whether permanently or merely temporarily no one can know for sure. However, it seems likely that they may return, simply because they have so many times in the last 2 or 3 million years. In the meantime, streams continue the endless task of shaping the landscape.

So far, human beings have contributed virtually nothing to that landscape. May it ever be so.

CHAPTER TWO

The Physiographic Regions

compiled by Rick Graetz

The physical attributes of the Bob Marshall Country are more easily understood if they are thought of by regions. The following land-form descriptions are generally based on river drainages. It would be extremely helpful to refer to the following three maps while reading through this section: Lewis and Clark Forest, Rocky Mountain Division; Flathead National Forest, North Half; and Flathead National Forest, South Half. Sources for these and other useful maps include:

Northern Regional Office
Box 7669
Missoula, MT 59807

Lewis & Clark National Forest
Box 871
Great Falls, MT 59403

Rocky Mountain Ranger District
Lewis and Clark National Forest
Box 340
Choteau, MT 59422

Flathead National Forest
Box 147
Kalispell, MT 59901

Augusta Information Station
Lewis and Clark National Forest
Box 365
Augusta, MT 59410

Seeley Lake Ranger District
Flathead National Forest
Drawer G
Seeley Lake, MT 59868

Helena National Forest
Drawer 10014
Helena, MT 59626

Swan Lake Ranger Station
Flathead National Forest
P.O. Box 438
Bigfork, MT 59911

Hungry Horse Ranger District
Flathead National Forest
Hungry Horse, MT 59919

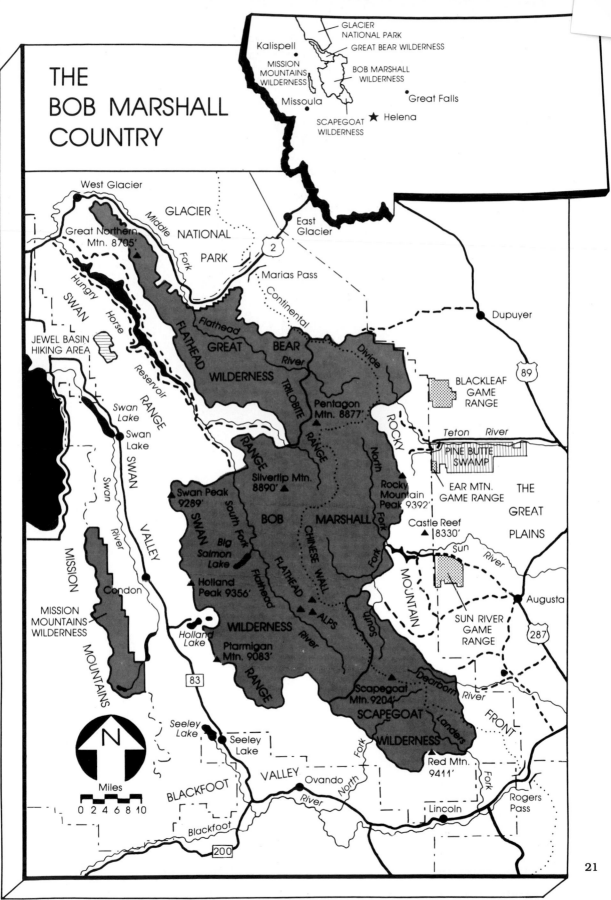

THE BOB MARSHALL COUNTRY

GLACIER NATIONAL PARK
GREAT BEAR WILDERNESS
Kalispell
MISSION MOUNTAINS WILDERNESS
BOB MARSHALL WILDERNESS
Missoula
Great Falls
SCAPEGOAT WILDERNESS
★ Helena

West Glacier
GLACIER NATIONAL PARK
Great Northern Mtn. 8705'
Middle Fork
East Glacier
2
Marias Pass
Continental
Hungry Horse Reservoir
SWAN
Flathead
GREAT BEAR WILDERNESS
Flathead River
Divide
Dupuyer
89
JEWEL BASIN HIKING AREA
RANGE
TRILOBITE RANGE
Pentagon Mtn. 8877'
BLACKLEAF GAME RANGE
Teton River
PINE BUTTE SWAMP
Swan Lake
RANGE
Silvertip Mtn. 8890'
North Fork
Rocky Mountain Peak 9392'
EAR MTN. GAME RANGE
THE
Swan Lake
Swan Peak 9289'
South Fork
BOB
MARSHALL
Castle Reef 8330'
GREAT
SWAN
Big Salmon Lake
CHINESE WALL
Sun River
PLAINS
Swan River
VALLEY
Condon
Holland Peak 9356'
FLATHEAD
Sun River
MOUNTAIN
Augusta
MISSION
Holland Lake
WILDERNESS
Flathead River
ALPS
SUN RIVER GAME RANGE
287
MISSION MOUNTAINS WILDERNESS
83
Ptarmigan Mtn. 9083'
RANGE
Smith Fork
Dearborn River
FRONT
MOUNTAINS
Seeley Lake
Scapegoat Mtn. 9204'
SCAPEGOAT
Landers Fork
N
Seeley Lake
WILDERNESS
Red Mtn. 9411'
Rogers Pass
Miles
0 2 4 6 8 10
BLACKFOOT
VALLEY
Ovando
Blackfoot River
North Fork
Lincoln
Blackfoot
200

Map by Ed Madej — Great Divide Graphics

9,392' Rocky Mountain Peak on the left looking at the end of the road up the South Fork of the Teton Canyon. The trail from here leads over Headquarters Peak just below Rocky Mountain Peak's north shoulder. Rocky Mountain Peak is the highest peak in the Rocky Mountain Front and in the Bob Marshall Wilderness proper. U.S. Forest Service photo.

Looking down Bruce Creek (top) towards the east from above Corrugate Ridge. Bruce Creek flows into the North Fork of the Teton River. U.S. Forest Service photo.

Caribou Peak (bottom) in the Scapegoat Country. U.S. Forest Service photo.

At right, the wild Middle Fork of the Flathead River in the Great Bear Wilderness. Dale Burke photo.

24

Rocky Mountain Front

The Rocky Mountain Front is perhaps the most prominent and impressive physical feature in Montana. Simply put, it is where the prairie ends and the mountains begin. No zone of transition here of gently and slowly rising foothills; mountain wall wastes no space in making its presence felt. For more than 100 miles it juts up in one mass directly from the rolling plains. On a clear day, the peaks, walls, reefs and ridges of the Front may be seen from 100 miles away.

This mountain front, sometimes called the Sawtooth Range, is an explicit view of a segment of the overthrust belt as a person travels Montana Highway 89 from its junction with Montana 200 to East Glacier.

It is fitting then that such a magnificent geologic structure serves as the eastern sentinel of the Bob Marshall country. The spectacular limestone fault scarps of the Front, rising more than 1,000', are the gates to the magnificent wildlands beyond. A few roads intrude a short way into the deep canyons providing access to wilderness trails. The sights of jagged reefs, rushing streams and towering peaks are only clues as to what the footpaths offer. And what a hint: They are some of the finest mountain views anywhere.

As if the scenery weren't enough, the Rocky Mountain Front is rich in wildlife, and makes a home for many species that have disappeared elsewhere. The largest populations of grizzly bear, bighorn sheep and wolverine south of Canada roam here and in the wilderness to the west. Assessments by the Forest Service show that much of the Front serves as critical grizzly habitat. Indeed, this area is the only place in the nation where the big bears still venture out to the prairie as they did when Lewis and Clark explored Montana. In the spring the grizzlies feed on the new vegetation in the aspen wetlands just east of the mountains.

A few Rocky Mountain grey wolves frequent the narrow canyons of the northern Front Range. West slope cutthroat trout, for the most part, found only on the west side of the Continental Divide, inhabit, in small numbers, some of the streams in the region. The reefs and walls provide sanctuary for bald and golden eagles, prairie falcons and peregrines.

The Rocky Mountain Front lies east of the Continental Divide and hence it is drier, windier and colder than the wilderness west of the Divide. Vegetation then is more sparse, providing for ample open country and big views. Some of the canyons are timbered, but most of the ridges are barren as are the hillsides, especially those facing south and west. Fires and flooding have also opened up the land. In 1964 and 1975 flood waters, resulting from a heavy snowpack and sudden June warming and rains, rampaged down the Sun, Teton, Birch and other drainages, leaving behind an enormous impact.

In spite of all this natural wealth that visually overwhelms other values, there have been proposals for development along the Front. The timber is, for the most part, uneconomical to harvest. But leasing applications for oil and gas exploration criss-cross the Front. Those of us dedicated to the Bob believe that it is appalling for the Forest Service to even consider exploration for oil and gas since what small amounts of natural gas may be trapped in the underlying rocks, would probably only be enough to supply the nation's demands for two months. The exploiters are the only beneficiaries of such development and the nation would be cheated forever of a unique natural area. At the time of this writing, most of these proposals have been held off, and we can only hope that the more responsible and sensible heads in the Forest Service, the agency managing these lands, prevail.

The areas with designated wilderness status are safe; however, much of the Rocky Mountain Front is only de facto wilderness. These areas await formal protection that the U.S. Congress can give, acting on proposals from various citizen organizations.

For a further look at the Rocky Mountain Front sector of the Bob Marshall country, it is helpful to consider it as five sub-regions.

Two Medicine-Badger

The first region starts in the north and covers the land between Glacier Park's southern boundary and the North Fork of Birch Creek. While most of the Rocky Mountain Front consists of big peaks and deep canyons, this segment includes the broad glacial valley of the South Fork of the Two Medicine River. Most of the peaks are part of Two Medicine Ridge, and with the exception of those near Birch Creek, are lower and less rugged than those farther south.

Badger Creek

Flowing north-northeast from the Continental Divide to the prairie, is another major drainage. Two Medicine, which starts in a meadow between Kyo Crag and Bullshoe Mountain, also flows north-northeast. Both are part of the Marias River system and offer fair fishing.

A grouping of peaks, just to the north of the North Fork of Birch Creek, is very inviting to climb. They are: 8,095' Family Peak, 8,282' Scarface Mountain, 8,376' Morningstar Mountain, 8,054' Spotted Eagle Mountain and 7,923' Curly Bear Mountain. These peaks are seldom visited, yet access is easy via the trail up Birch Creek from Swift Reservoir to Badger Pass and then down Badger Creek. The Badger trail continues to Highway 2.

Heart Butte

On the edge of the Front is a prominent landmark that was a place Indians scaled to seek visions.

Birch Creek Country

The next geographical sector takes in the terrain from the North Fork of Birch Creek south to a divide that tops out at Corrugate Ridge on the Continental Divide, heading northeast over Mount Patrick Gass, Bloody Hill, Bennie Hill and Hurricane Mountain. The Continental Divide is its western boundary.

It's a popular hiking area, owing to its varied and spectacular scenery and easy access from Swift Reservoir. The North, Middle and South Forks of Birch Creek drain the country. The canyons are narrow in most places, but easy to negotiate. 8,625' Mount Patrick Gass, named after a member of the Lewis and Clark Expedition, is a great climb, and is accessed by way of a pass up Crazy Creek, a tributary of the South Fork of Birch Creek. It may also be reached from the North Fork of the Teton and Bruce Creek to the south.

Swift Reservoir is hemmed in by two big walls, Major Steele Backbone on the north and Walling Reef to the south.

Teton River Drainage

The region south of the Birch Creek country to a divide that runs between Rocky Mountain Peak and Ear Mountain offers perhaps the most diverse recreation, coupled with mountain splendor on the Front. Here the mountains are big and awesome, with great relief.

Two roads forking from the main road from Choteau work their way into the Front until they reach the wilderness buffer zone. One goes up the North Fork of the Teton River, and ends near the confluence of the North and West Forks of the Teton. The other follows the South Fork of the Teton to the Headquarters Pass trailhead. The scenery en route is unparalleled and shows the best of the Rocky Mountain Front.

The North Fork road is plowed in winter to Teton Pass ski area, a small gem of a ski mountain, owned and operated by a private group from Choteau. The scenery and the friendliness of the people make this a worthwhile place to visit. The remaining three miles of the road, down to the West Fork Ranger Station, remains unplowed and is set aside as a snowmobile play area, as are other places below the ski area. Forest Service campgrounds are found at the end of each of these roads.

Because of the plowed road, good ski touring is possible deep into the wilderness. This area is probably the best possibility of high-country touring of any along the Front.

For the hiker and climber, the trail from the West Fork goes up to Teton Pass on the divide and opens up the headwaters country of the Middle Fork of the Flathead. Mount Patrick Gass, mentioned earlier, is reached from the West Fork, as is 8,855' Mount Wright.

The South Fork road leads to one of the main routes into the Sun River country and the Chinese Wall, and the trail to Headquarters Pass. This trail is also the route to 9,392' Rocky Mountain Peak, the highest peak on the Rocky Mountain Front. This beautiful mountain, by virtue of its elevation, reveals much of the Bob Marshall country on all sides for the climber. The peaks of Glacier are visible far to the north as is the Swan Crest far to the west. And on a clear day, the outlying prairie ranges, some 100 miles away, come into view.

Teton Peak, 8,416', another big Front peak is reached by the trail to 7,263' Route Creek Pass, or by a rugged cross-country walk from below Teton Pass ski area.

Ear Mountain, 8,380', is the big sentinel guarding the South Fork of the Teton Canyon and the Ear Mountain Game Range.

Gibson Lake, Ford and Wood Creeks

The divide between Rocky Mountain Peak and Ear Mountain separates the Teton from the Deep Creek drainage and the next area of the Front. From this divide south to the road

The road to Benchmark. Wood Lake is in the center of the photograph. U.S. Forest Service photo.

29

Above Route Creek Pass looking at the north face of Old Baldy. Rocky Mountain Peak is the next high summit to the south of Old Baldy. U.S. Forest Service photo.

through Wood Canyon to Benchmark is another sector offering varied recreation, because of the presence of several roads and Gibson Lake. This country is reached out of Augusta.

The centerpiece is five-and-one-half-mile-long Gibson Reservoir, the Sun River impounded by Gibson Dam. Gibson is too cold for swimming but offers good boat fishing, especially in the spring. The road from Augusta goes to the lake near the dam and a Forest Service campground. A trail takes off from here into the wilderness through the canyons of the North and South Forks of the Sun.

The peaks and gulches on the north side of the lake serve as major winter range for a large bighorn sheep population, and whitetail deer and elk.

Deep Creek Canyon, to the north, is very scenic and impressive. Access is best gained by hiking the various gulches, with Blacktail offering the only through trail. Deep Creek flows to the prairie, but private ground and rough roads must be negotiated on the east.

A scenic road, open only part of the year, goes south from Gibson Dam up Beaver Creek, down Willow Creek and back to Augusta. From the same road, west of Augusta, another road heads to Benchmark Ranger Station through Ford and Wood Creek Canyons.

Benchmark is perhaps the most heavily used trailhead into the Bob Marshall Wilderness, especially by horse parties. Trails from here also lead to the Scapegoat Wilderness. The trail up the South Fork of the Sun and the West Fork of the South Fork is a good route to White River Pass and the Chinese Wall. Packers also use it to reach the White River and the South Fork of the Flathead.

Renshaw Mountain, 8,264', is reached by trail from the Benchmark area, and 8,245' Fairview Mountain, reached from the Beaver-Willow Creek road, are good climbs. Both peaks give the hiker an excellent perspective on the overthrust geology of the area. The view defines definite north-south alignment of the long gulches and shows off the sheer east faces and sloping west sides of the reefs and ridges.

Sawtooth Ridge, 8,175', and Castle Reef, 7,005', on the north and south sides of the Sun, are the gates to the Sun River Canyon. The Sun River Game Range, wintering grounds for a large elk herd, is below the east wall of Sawtooth.

Dearborn River-Falls Creek

The southern-most segment of the Rocky Mountain Front takes in the country between the Wood-Ford Creek Road south to the Continental Divide and Lewis and Clark Pass. The Continental Divide borders it on the west. Roads from Augusta up Smith Creek and Elk Creek, and the Dearborn River from a road off of Highway 200, provide access.

The Smith Creek and Elk Creek roads lead to Scapegoat Wilderness trailheads. 6,004' Elk Pass, a few miles from the end of the Elk Creek Road, is the take-off point for a trail to the top of 8,579' Steamboat Mountain. For a view of most of the Rocky Mountain Front and the wilderness, the mountain offers the best of any. It is farther east than the other peaks and reefs of the Front, enabling the climber to see the collision point of the prairie and mountains.

The Dearborn road ends at a church camp several miles to the west of Bean Lake. From here the trail follows the river to the Welcome Creek area and eventually to the Dearborn headwaters below Scapegoat Mountain.

The country to the south of the Dearborn is called the Falls Creek-Silver King area. Trails lead in from the Dearborn road and from Lewis and Clark Pass. Caribou Peak, 8,773', on the Continental Divide is at the head of the several forks of Falls Creek.

I've covered the Rocky Mountain Front in more detail than the other geographic regions of the Bob Marshall country for several reasons. First, it is my favorite place of all the wild country I've ever been privileged to see. The combination of beautiful rolling prairie, sheer mountain majesty, awesome canyons and such a wide expanse is unsurpassed. The roads that venture into the canyons give those who aren't able to, or choose not to, ride horseback or walk, the opportunity to see all that the wilderness traveler observes. It gives these people a touch of wildness on a grand scale. If formal wilderness designation comes to the wild lands near and beyond these roads, the roads will remain open, and what the visitor sees will be further enhanced.

The only way we can improve on what we see now from the roads and trails is to designate the areas deserving of it, wilderness status. Some of the ranchers in the area would like to see the country remain as is without wilderness protection. That would be perfectly desirable except that administrations in Washington and the Forest Service change and we can't be assured of protection forever. It must be emphasized that any gas potential or timber value is minuscule compared to the value that wildness gives to the country, both in real economic terms and multiple-use values of recreation, watershed protection, wildlife habitat and grazing.

And indeed the country in a wild state is valuable. Montana sportsmen have helped increase the wildlife population of the Front with the purchase of three game ranges: the Sun River Range west of Augusta near the mouth of the Sun River Canyon, Ear Mountain Game Range west of Choteau and just south of the South Fork of the Teton Canyon, and Blackleaf Game Range west of Bynum by the mouth of Blackleaf Canyon.

Thanks to these efforts, and those of the ranchers along the Front, the elk population is ten times greater, and the mule deer herd 20 times larger than at the turn of the century, and the big horn sheep population is a national resource.

To further enhance wildlife habitat on the Front the non-profit group, The Nature Conservancy, began in 1978 to assemble one of the largest and most stunning of its sanctuary projects, the Pine Butte Swamp Preserve. Using carefully assembled biological data, The Conservancy has identified for protection some 50,000 acres of foothills, prairie, swamp and river flood plain.

Keying its project on the threatened grizzly bear, The Nature Conservancy will save what is thought to be the last regularly used prairie habitat for the great bear. In the course of that protection effort, essential habitat for many other species of plants and animals will be secure for generations to come.

Recognizing that the task of protecting the Front Range necessitates combined private and public action, The Conservancy works with ranchers, public- and private-interest organizations, state and federal agencies to find agreeable mixes of land ownership, use and management for the Front Range. The success of the Pine Butte Swamp project bodes well for similar efforts all along the Front. Ideally, The Nature Conservancy approach could result in effective noncontroversial protection for key lands from Canada to Highway 200. The intermingled private and public land holdings managed capably and intelligently would then complement the wild land and wildlife values that are now exposed to a host of development threats.

Sun River Drainages

The North Fork of the Sun, headwatering at 7,800' Sun River Pass on the Continental Divide, drains a portion of the west side of the Rocky Mountain Front and the mass of mountains just to the east of the divide between Sun River Pass and Gibson Lake.

Sun River Pass, incidentally, separates the Sun drainage from that of the Middle Fork of the Flathead. It is 30 miles from the pass to where the North Fork enters Gibson Lake.

Timber is heavier and open spaces scarce in the upper reaches of the North Fork. As one goes south, meadows and big parks become more prevalent. Gates Park (formerly called Cates after an early day homesteader) is the first big open stretch. It is the site of a Forest Service back-country guard station and presents good views of the surrounding mountains. The valley of the North Fork, perhaps the widest in the Bob Marshall Country, begins to spread out here. Below Gates Park the timber comes back, but soon other meadows are reached such as Biggs Creek Flat, Two Shacks Flat and Circle Creek. Before wilderness designation, cattle grazed these areas. Now with the cattle gone, trees are closing in on the smaller parks.

From Circle Creek south, there are few trees in the bottom lands and on the slopes to the east. This region is habitat, to within a couple of miles north of Gibson Lake, for the big Sun River elk herd (discussed in the wildlife section).

The mountains on the west side of the Sun River, all the way across to the West Fork of the South Fork of the Sun and the Continental Divide, are part of the Sun River Game Preserve. No hunting is allowed in the preserve. Many times I have trekked through the country, either on skis or foot and witnessed herds of elk stampeding all around me to cross the river to the game preserve where they knew they'd be safe.

From the North Fork Valley and Elk Ridge, several impressive mountain peaks may be viewed. From north to south, they are 8,878' Slategoat Mountain, Sheep Mountain, and 8,868' Prairie Reef. To climb Slategoat, it is necessary to trek cross country, but a trail goes to the top of Prairie Reef from the West Fork of the South Fork of the Sun River. It's a tough six-mile climb but worth it for the views it offers of the Chinese Wall, the Sun River country and the Rocky Mountain Front to the east.

Two well-used trails start out of the North Fork of the Sun country heading to the Chinese Wall. From Gates Park a trail runs up Hoxsey and Rock Creek to Spotted Bear Pass to Larch

a

b

(a) Looking downstream along the South Fork of the Flathead River near Woodfir Creek. U.S. Forest Service photo. (b) From the Pearl Basin area looking toward the peaks of the Flathead Alps. The photo was taken in 1937. U.S. Forest Service photo. (c) Big Salmon Lake at its outlet in what was then the South Fork of the Flathead Primitive Area when this photo was taken in 1934 by K.D. Swan. U.S. Forest Service photo. (d) The South Fork of the Flathead River at a point about ¼ mile above Big Prairie Ranger Station. The photo was taken in 1928 by Henry Thol. U.S. Forest Service photo.

c

d

35

Above, Hungry Horse Lake and Great Northern Mountain in the Flathead Range of the Great Bear Wilderness. Photo taken by Danny On in 1965. Hungry Horse Dam impounds the South Fork of the Flathead River in Hungry Horse Lake. The lake itself is outside of the wilderness boundary. U.S. of the wilderness boundary. U.S. Forest Service photo.

Looking south (below) down Hungry Horse Lake from above Hungry Horse Dam. Bureau of Reclamation photo.

Near the beginning of the South Fork of the Flathead River drainage above the Danaher River. The Danaher Meadows are in the middle of the photograph. The mountains in the distance are part of the Swan Range. Rick Graetz photo.

Left top: above Lonesome Creek looking down the South Fork of Badger Creek in the Two Medicine Badger Region. U.S. Forest Service photo.

Left bottom: the road up the North Fork of the Teton River and Mount Lockhart and Teton Pass ski area. The ski area is outside the wilderness boundary. U.S. Forest Service photo.

The Falls Creek area (above). The Continental Divide is on the right. U.S. Forest Service photo.

Hill Pass and the northern end of the wall. From Two Shacks Flat, the Moose Creek trail goes directly to the center section of the wall. This is a favorite horsepacker route. Just above the head of Gibson Lake and the confluence of the North and South Forks of the Sun River is Medicine Springs. The Klick family has an inholding here for a guest ranch and the spring is now used for their guests, but at one time Indians traveled to this area to use the water for healing purposes. Hence the name, Medicine Springs.

The mountain mass south of Moose Creek and on the west side of the North Fork of the Sun separates this drainage from that of the West Fork of the South Fork of the Sun. The West Fork heads in a small, swampy lake below an outlying ridge of the Chinese Wall near Cliff Mountain, the highest point on the Chinese Wall. From here it tumbles down a narrow steep canyon on its 13-mile journey to the confluence of the South Fork of the Sun. Below Indian Point, the site of a Forest Service Guard Station, the river is an intermittent mix of open meadows and forest. Trails from the West Fork, in the vicinity of Indian Point, lead to White River Pass and the south end of the Chinese Wall, as well as to Pearl Basin on the Continental Divide.

The South Fork of the Sun River has its headwaters near Scapegoat Mountain at 8,500 feet on the Continental Divide. As it flows on its 25-mile journey to Gibson Lake, it passes Benchmark and one of the more popular routes into the Bob Marshall country. For the most part, the canyon is timbered and rocky, but downstream from its confluence with the West Fork is Pretty Prairie, a series of big meadows.

From Benchmark a trail works its way up the South Fork of the Sun into the Scapegoat country and 9,790' Flint Mountain. This same trail is a good route into the Danaher Meadows on the west side of the Continental Divide. It winds over some of the high points of the Scapegoat Plateau. Another route from this trail goes over 7,444' Observation Pass into the Danaher.

Continental Divide Ranges

The Continental Divide commences its journey south into the heart of the Bob Marshall country at 5,206' Marias Pass. From this point on Glacier National Park's southern border, no road will again cross the divide for more than 145 miles until it reaches 5,609' Rogers Pass and Montana Highway 200. An unofficial Continental Divide trail stays with the divide for about 168 miles. In many areas, especially the southern end, bushwhacking is required. Forest Service maps, USGS guides and inquiries to local Forest Service offices would help in planning a divide trek. Sources for information are listed elsewhere in the book.

The peaks along the divide aren't the highest in the wilderness complex. In the northern third of the area the highest points are 8,590' Mount Field, near Badger Pass, and 8,412' Kevan Mountain, near Switchback Pass and Dean Lake. Along the central divide, the highest elevations are 8,310' Hahn Peak on what is called the north wall; 8,789' Redhead Peak, east of Spotted Bear Pass; 8,576' Cliff Mountain and 8,396' Haystack Mountain, the two highest points on the Chinese Wall; 8,700' Junction Mountain, in the Flathead Alps and above Pearl Basin; and 8,744' Twin Peaks above Ahorn Basin. On the southern crest the tallest summits are 8,698' Sugarloaf, north of Observation Pass; 8,572' Triple Divide; 8,523' Observation Point; 9,079' Flint Mountain and 9,204' Scapegoat Mountain. All four are part of the Scapegoat massif. In the Lincoln back country 8,611' Crow Peak, above Carmichael Basin, and 8,773' Caribou Peak are the tallest summits.

Some of the Bob's most prominent features straddle the Continental Divide. Big River Meadows is one of these, so named because Gateway Creek begins here as one of the headwater streams of the big Middle Fork of the Flathead. These huge meadows offer a rare place where you walk into a mountain pass, rather than climb up to it. Gateway Pass, a favorite Indian route across the divide, is at the eastern edge of the meadows.

Strawberry Creek, starting out as a spring at Badger Pass on the divide, joins with Gateway Creek to help form the Middle Fork.

The Big River Meadows, Gateway and Badger Pass areas are reached by trails up the North and South Forks of Birch Creek from Swift Reservoir.

Corrugate Ridge, a four-mile-long limestone wall, is another divide landmark, and is reached by way of Teton Pass or Bruce Creek from road's end at the West Fork Teton Ranger Station.

The Kevan Mountain-Switchback Pass area of the Continental Divide, deep in the wilderness, is very impressive and is reached by hard walking from the West Fork Teton area, Birch Creek trails or from Spotted Bear on the South Fork of the Flathead.

The crown jewel of the Bob Marshall, the Chinese Wall, dominates almost 13 miles of the divide country. This geologic wonder is the classic example of overthrust geology. On its east face the wall towers up to 1,000' above the meadows below. The west side slopes for several miles down to the White River. Larch Hill Pass, 7,702', on the north, offers the best view of the escarpment. The meadows below White River Pass, the wall's southern terminus, also open good views of parts of the east face.

The country below the wall consists mostly of lush open meadows. In the Moose Creek area a huge fire has opened up the adjacent hillsides, giving further accent to this spectacular uplift. The top of the Chinese Wall, and much of the upper west slope, is free of dense tree cover. Many seashell fossils are evident atop the cliffs.

In the fall, the amphitheater of the wall and adjoining high meadows are gathering ground for elk.

There is only one relatively easy route up the wall's east side between the two passes. Outfitters who frequent the area call it Trick Pass. Half of the fun in using this pass is finding it. Walking the wall is a great experience.

The Chinese Wall is well into the heart of the wilderness, and many trails lead to it. The most popular routes are out of Benchmark, Headquarters Pass and Gibson Lake from the east, Spotted Bear on the north and the Danaher country to the south. The most direct routes are from the east side of the divide.

A close second to the Chinese Wall as a spectacular geologic masterpiece is the Scapegoat Mountain complex. At 9,204', Scapegoat Mountain is the highest peak in the Bob Marshall Country sector of the Continental Divide. The mountain itself is is only a big bump on top of a three- to four-mile-long limestone plateau. The walls are sheer on almost all sides with access to the top restricted to the Green Fork drainage on the east and a few places on the west side. The top of the plateau is somewhat flat and then rises on the north to 9,079' Flint Mountain.

The massif is dotted with caves and is a favorite of serious cavers. In the Green Fork drainage, a stream comes out of the wall like a faucet, and behind it a cave is reported to be about two miles long. A word of warning is necessary here: These caves are not for amateurs to explore; they are dangerous.

Half Moon Park, below the northeast side of Scapegoat Mountain, is a beautiful place, and as a fire has burned through the area, is open to all views. Below a ridge to the south of Half Moon, the Dearborn River begins flowing to the prairie and the Missouri River.

Access to Scapegoat is usually from the east by way of Elk Pass, the Dearborn River, Smith Creek or the Benchmark area. From the south and west side, approaches to the Scapegoat Mountain and Plateau are from the Danaher, the North Fork of the Blackfoot River and the Lincoln back country. The Dobroda Creek headwater area, reached by trail from the North Fork Blackfoot Valley, offers one of the better ways to climb Scapegoat from the west.

Many passes cross the Continental Divide Range. Some of them are: Muskrat Pass, 5,974', coming up from the Badger Creek and the Two Medicine River drainage to Beaver Lake and to another crossing about two miles away; 6,278' Badger Pass and the Middle Fork of the Flathead headwaters; Gateway Pass, 6,478', an historic pass used by the Indians crossing from the west to the buffalo hunting grounds, reached by going up the South Fork of Birch Creek, or from the Middle Fork country; Teton Pass, 7775', reached from the West Fork Teton River, and leading to Bowl Creek and the Middle Fork of the Flathead; Switchback Pass, 7,767', on the divide between the Spotted Bear River and Sun River headwaters; Spotted Bear Pass, 6,721', reached by way of Rock Creek to the east and the Spotted Bear River on the north side; Larch Hill Pass, 7,702', the north end of the Chinese Wall; White River Pass, 7,626', the southern end of the wall and part of a major route across the Bob; Camp Creek Pass, 7,200', reached from the Danaher and providing access to Pearl Basin; Observation Pass, 7,444', a crossing from the South Fork of the Sun to the upper Danaher Basin. South of Scapegoat Mountain, a few trails cross the divide on lower unnamed passes.

Peak and pass elevations and locations have been listed to provide points of reference. The Continental Divide Range is for the most part seldom visited along most of its route. To see it in these areas requires bushwhacking and some steep climbing. If you are in shape, have good equipment, know how to use a map and compass, and know what you are doing, the rewards are well worth the effort. This is pristine country, however. Practice no-trace camping and remember much of the area provides a summer sanctuary for wildlife.

a

b

(a) The Scapegoat Massif and Scapegoat Mountain. Halfmoon Park is the area to the left of the wall. The drainage of the Green Fork is on the right. U.S. Forest Service photo.

(b) Bighorn Peak and Lake in the Scapegoat country. U.S. Forest Service photo.

c

d

(c) Triple Divide Peak north of Scapegoat Mountain. U.S. Forest Service photo.

(d) Crow Peak and the Carmichael Basin in the Scapegoat Country. U.S. Forest Service photo.

The Middle Fork of the Flathead Drainage

Old timers called Montana's wildest waterway "Big River." Today it is known as the Middle Fork of the Flathead. Indeed it is big; the river and its tributaries dominate the Great Bear Wilderness. The drainage basin is bordered on the east and parts of the south by the Continental Divide and Elk Ridge, some high country near Pentagon Mountain. The Flathead Range flanks the west and the southern boundary, and Glacier Park, the north.

The big river begins its journey at the confluence of Strawberry and Bowl Creeks and flows for 46 miles through the wilderness to Bear Creek at Highway 2. For its first 15 miles it is in a very remote timbered valley until reaching Schafer Meadows. Schafer is somewhat of an island in the wilderness. It features a landing strip that has been kept open as part of an agreement struck when the Great Bear Wilderness was created. From Schafer north, the stream cuts through sedimentary rock cliffs that soar to steep mountain slopes above. En route it varies between wild and dangerous waters to calm pools. The floods of 1964 and 1975 have swept clean many of the log jams, but the water is still as dangerous in some areas.

This stretch from Schafer downstream offers some of the best and most spectacular whitewater floating in Montana. A segment somewhere between three to four miles long, below Spruce Park, is a favorite of whitewater enthusiasts. In this area alone, the river drops more than 40 feet per mile. The Middle Fork in its entirety offers the steepest drop per mile of any of the forks of the Flathead River. It starts at 5,500 feet at Strawberry Creek and falls to 3,800 feet at Bear Creek. Its average drop is 35 feet per mile in the wilderness stretch, compared to 15 feet for the North Fork and 19 feet for the South Fork of the Flathead. (These figures come from an outstanding book, *Great Bear, Wild River* by Dale A. Burk.)

The conditions for floating are best in May and June, and sometimes early July. That is, if you like your water fast, as this is the peak of the runoff season. It is best to check conditions with the U.S. Forest Service for the time you plan to go.

Fishing on the Middle Fork is better the farther you get from Schafer Meadows. Easy access to the meadows has virtually destroyed the fishing in that area.

Many tributaries add to the flow of the Middle Fork, but some are especially noteworthy. Gateway Creek heads in the Big River Meadows just off the Continental Divide and flows through Gateway Gorge, a towering limestone wall created by water and wind erosion that rises more than 1,000 feet above the stream. Gateway eventually joins Strawberry Creek, which starts as a trickle just below Badger Pass on the Continental Divide.

Bowl Creek starts on the Continental Divide at Teton Pass and rushes down a steep canyon to join Strawberry Creek, forming the Middle Fork. It is reached by way of the West Fork of the Teton over Teton Pass and also from the trails coming down Strawberry Creek.

Clack Creek travels through some of the Bob's most scenic country. It commences at Dean and Trilobite Lakes. The Trilobite Range, towering above these creeks, is a massive land form that vies with the river itself for attention. It runs the full stretch of the Clack and Dean Creek drainage as those waters make their way to the Middle Fork of the Flathead at Gooseberry Park. The Trilobite Range, starting just above Dean Lake, was named after the fossils found in it. 8,877' Pentagon Mountain, one of the most beautiful summits in the Bob Marshall country, is at the southern tip of the range. The range, or ridge, heads north until it runs out at Schafer Meadows, ten miles away.

Basin Creek, heading just below Pentagon Mountain, is part of the Middle Fork of the Flathead drainage but it flows east before joining Bowl Creek and running north to the main river. Do not believe the maps that show a trail up it, because no trail exists, except in the lower portions. I have hiked the area several times, but the traces of the trail are very few and the going can be quite rough. And, it is grizzly country.

Dolly Varden Creek, named after the fish found in it, is on the west side of the Trilobite Range, with headwaters below Elk Ridge and Pentagon Mountain. The open sections in this country and some of the others on the east side of the Trilobite Range are an exception; for the most part, the headwaters country of the Middle Fork and its tributaries is heavily timbered.

Downstream from Schafer Meadows, the creeks coming in add to the water supply but they are in more heavily timbered regions than those on the south and aren't as long as the upper streams.

The main Middle Fork's upper reaches are accessed by the trails just mentioned. However, the Big River Trail follows the entire length of the river to Highway 2. In quite a few places it is well above the river, high up on the cliffs, opening up some great views of the canyon. Access to the lower segments of the river is gained via Granite Creek from a road off of Highway 2 and Morrison Creek, reached by the same road.

All of the Middle Fork drainage is very mountainous, but most of the peaks are less than 8,000 feet. However, as the river elevations continue to decrease, the peaks become more imposing because of the great relief.

It is important to note that much of the high country in the upper reaches of the Middle Fork of the Flathead and Great Bear Wilderness Region is very wild and remote and provides habitat for the great grizzly bear. It's something to keep in mind when traveling here.

The Central Ranges

This area, like the Chinese Wall, is the heart of the Bob Marshall country. It takes in the Spotted Bear drainage, just to the south of the Flathead Range, and is bordered by the Chinese Wall to the east and the South Fork of the Flathead River on the west. It culminates at Camp Creek Pass on the Continental Divide, south of the Chinese Wall. It also includes the country of the White River.

The Spotted Bear River starts on the Continental Divide below Spotted Bear Pass and is fed by several other notable tributaries including Wall Creek and Silvertip Creeks, whose headwaters are below Silvertip Mountain. The Wall Creek Cliffs are an interesting geologic formation — nearly as high as the Chinese Wall — in the headwaters area of the Spotted Bear. Bungalow Mountain (8,140') near the Wall Creek Cliffs, is a good climb by trail from the same headwaters area, and is visited by few.

Silvertip Mountain (8,890'), just to the west of the Wall Creek Cliffs, is considered by many to be the sentinel of the Bob Marshall country. Visible from almost any point in this big wilderness complex, it is a favorite of cavers and is reported to contain one of the deepest caves in the United States as well as more than five miles of lateral caves. The Silvertip area, named after one of the grizzly bear's nicknames, provides excellent summer bear habitat.

The White River, a major tributary of the South Fork of the Flathead, is born on the west slopes of Silvertip Mountain. The drainage is hemmed in on the west by a ridge of peaks going south from Silvertip Peak and by the Wall Creek Cliffs and the Larch Hill Pass ridge coming off of the south end of the Chinese Wall, and the wall itself, to the east. It's a very definite basin that shows evidence a glacier had started in a cirque below Silvertip Mountain and carved out a perfect U-shaped valley for much of the White River's route. The sloping west side of the Chinese Wall begins its rise from the White River bottomlands. From below Silvertip Mountain the shallow and wide White River flows for 20 miles on its way to the South Fork of the Flathead. It flows south initially, and then turns west. The smaller South Fork of the White River joins the main stream just below White River Pass and the southern end of the Chinese Wall. This lower end of the river flows along one of the major routes crossing the Bob Marshall.

Geologically the upper valley of the White River is unusual compared to most of the Bob Marshall country, because of a phenomenon called the White River Syncline. Here the east slope of the mountains above the river's west side drops gently westward, whereas in most of the Bob the peaks and ridges rise sharply on the east and gradually on the west.

The lower White River up to Needle Falls provides good fishing. The falls are high and serve as a fish barrier. Some of the upper stretches are good for portions of the year, but tend to dry up later in the summer. The group of mountains above the White River to the west offers an alternate route to the South Fork of the Flathead via a trail over Pagoda Pass on the south side of 8,030' Pagoda Mountain. The main trail goes down Helen Creek. A cross-country route, above Damnation Creek, with a trail visible part of the way, would be followed with difficulty.

Pagoda is a good climb as are 8,804' Helen Mountain and 8,483' Lone Butte. The slopes of these peaks, as well as much of the upper parts of the White River country, are open. Excellent views are the rule.

From above the prairie looking up the South Fork of the Teton River Canyon on the left and the North Fork of the Teton River to the right. Headquarters Pass is in the saddle to the left just below Rocky Mountain Peak. Teton Peak rises in the center of the photograph. Pentagon Mountain is the pyramid-like peak on the right horizon.

The rugged and glacier-scoured peaks towering over the White River to the south are called the Flathead Alps. These mountains are some of the most spectacular in the Bob Marshall country. Junction Mountain (8,700') on the Continental Divide is the highest in the range. All the other peaks are less than 8,000 feet, but as seen from the South Fork of the Flathead, they rise several thousand feet. Trails meander to them from the South Fork and the Danaher. Although they may be somewhat accessible from the White River trail, they are best reached from the South Fork drainage or by way of Pearl Basin and Camp Creek Pass, coming up from the West Fork of the South Fork of the Sun River.

Like many of the other high remote areas of the Bob Marshall country, this is prime grizzly-bear habitat. For your safety and out of respect for the bear, if you wish to wander in these high remote places, consider that this is the bear's home and avoid disturbing him. Plan to visit some of these areas in the winter or earlier in the year when the bear may be feeding at lower altitudes.

Flathead Range – Hungry Horse Lake Area

This region is bordered on the east by the Middle Fork of the Flathead drainage and on the west by the Swan Range and the west shore of Hungry Horse Lake. U.S. Highway 2 and Glacier Park border it on the north and the Spotted Bear River to the south.

The peaks of the Flathead Range, like many in the northern part of the Bob Marshall country, look much higher than they really are. Most are less than 8,000 feet, yet the relief in the area is more than 4,000 feet.

From Hungry Horse Lake, and also from parts of Highway 2, the two highest peaks, 8,705' Great Northern Mountain and 8,590' Mount Grant, are clearly visible. Close to each other and not all that far from roads, these are very tough climbs.

In winter, and maybe even summer, the best access to Great Northern Mountain is from the logging roads on the west side. This is the only safe way it can be climbed in the winter. Check with the Hungry Horse Ranger Station for details. A more scenic route for summer use is up Stanton Creek by way of beautiful Stanton Lake. However, the trail disappears in the upper parts and it is necessary to negotiate very steep brush-infested avalanche slopes. After leaving the brush, the climber faces steep rocky slopes to negotiate before reaching the glacier on the northeast side of the mountain.

Mount Grant is reached by Grant Creek from Highway 2.

There are other peaks in the Flathead Range, but they aren't as easily reached and it is necessary to do quite a bit of cross-country walking and bushwhacking.

Hungry Horse Reservoir is not a wilderness body of water as it is circumvented by a road and surrounded by many clear cuts. However, it is still part of the Bob Marshall country, providing access to the back country. The lake was formed when the South Fork of the Flathead River was dammed for a flood control project, completed in 1953.

The lake is 34 miles long and 3 to 4 miles across at its widest places. Boating is popular on Hungry Horse, but stumps found in the bays and near the islands can be hazardous. For this reason, and because of the cold water temperature, swimming and water skiing are not that popular here.

Gravel roads follow both shorelines and are narrow and winding; travel is slow at best. However, the roads reach several campgrounds, places to put in a boat and enjoy various scenic views, for those who can ignore the clear-cuts on the slopes above the lake. In spite of these shortcomings, Hungry Horse Lake is well worth seeing. These roads also lead to Spotted Bear Work Center and Ranger Station, a Forest Service complex. From there a road goes to Beaver Creek Campground and trails into the Spotted Bear River headwaters. Another road off the route to Spotted Bear leads to Meadow and Bunker Creeks. Trails from these roads head toward the South Fork of the Flathead, and beyond.

For more information on Hungry Horse Lake and boating possibilities, an address appears elsewhere in this book. Access is by way of Hungry Horse, Montana located on U.S. Highway 2 near the entrance to Glacier National Park at West Glacier, Montana. Roads along the lake are open only in the summer months.

Preceding page, top: the Chinese Wall from above Larch Hill Pass looking south, Rick Graetz; *bottom:* Bill Cunningham, Henry Loble, and Cathy Campbell from above Larch Hill Pass looking south along the Chinese Wall, Rick Graetz

This page, top: the Chinese Wall looking north toward Larch Hill Pass; Silvertip Mountain is to the left, Rick Graetz; *center:* from the top of the Chinese Wall looking north toward the Wall Creek Cliffs, Rick Graetz; *bottom:* from the top of the Chinese Wall looking southwest toward the White River country, Rick Graetz

Opposite page, top: the Chinese Wall from below Cliff Mountain looking north toward the head of Moose Creek, Rick Graetz; *bottom:* the Flathead Alps, to the south of the Chinese Wall, Rick Graetz

Opposite page, top: a trail winds through beargrass in the Great Bear Wilderness, Rick Graetz; *center:* climbing the east ridge of Rocky Mountain Peak looking toward Headquarters Peak on the left and Teton Peak in the distance on the right, Rick Graetz; *bottom:* backpackers camping below the east face of Rocky Mountain Peak, Rick Graetz *This page, top:* from the top of Rocky Mountain Peak, looking toward the North Fork of the Sun River country and beyond to the Chinese Wall. Rick Graetz; *bottom:* the west slopes of 9,392' Rocky Mountain Peak, the highest summit on the Rocky Mountain Front, Rick Graetz

Opposite page: from the top of Rocky Mountain Peak looking northeast down the valley of the Southfork of the Teton River and the peaks of the Rocky Mountain Front in the distance. Rick Graetz

This page, top: winter on the North Fork of the Teton River, Rick Graetz; bottom: waterfall below Headquarters Pass, Rick Graetz

Top: *mountain goats on Scapegoat Mountain. Gus Wolfe*
Bottom: *bull elk in the North Fork of the Sun River country. Bob Cooney*

Top: *young grizzly bear in the Bob Marshall country. Bill Lancaster*
Bottom: *moose. Gus Wolfe*

Above: *mountain lion cub. Gus Wolfe*
Opposite page, top: *band of Rocky Mountain bighorn sheep near Big George Gulch, Gus Wolfe;* **bottom:***elk herd on the Rocky Mountain Front, Gus Wolfe*

Bald eagle in the Sun River country. Bill Lancaster

Golden eagle and young on the Rocky Mountain Front. Gus Wolfe

Left: hunters along the trail in the heart of the Bob Marshall. Gus Wolfe
Below: Robert Casey hunting sheep in the Bob Marshall country. Gus Wolfe

Top: *the Skyline outfit heading out of the White River Valley. The west slopes of the Chinese Wall are in the distance. Rick Graetz*
Bottom: *looking north up the drainage of the White River toward Silvertip Peak on the left and the west slopes of the Chinese Wall on the right from above the Flathead Alps. Rick Graetz*

Mountain ash in the fall. Rick Graetz

The Danaher and the South Fork of the Flathead

Flowing for more than 70 miles, the Danaher and the South Fork of the Flathead drain much of the western sector of the Bob Marshall country. This river system is a fabulous wilderness experience for many people. Outfitters use it to make a living, and backpackers, horse parties and floaters enjoy all this wild, wilderness river offers. Fishing is excellent in this tranquil wilderness setting. The waterway begins on the lowest pass in the Bob Marshall country, the Dry Fork Flathead Divide at 5,400', and just below 8,002' Danaher Mountain. For five to seven miles, the Danaher flows through timbered country until it starts meandering through board meadows. The Danaher Meadows are the largest of these open areas. This was the site of an unsuccessful homesteading attempt before wilderness designation. Three miles north of the Danaher Meadows, the river enters what is simply called The Basin. Here Basin and Camp Creeks come together with the Danaher. This area was the site of an Indian battle over hunting rights.

After The Basin, the river flows through a canyon where it meets Youngs Creek. Here Youngs Creek and the Danaher form the South Fork of the Flathead River. Along these upper stretches there are many broad, grassy parks, some dotted here and there with yellow pine and stately ponderosa pine. The first of these is at Big Prairie, the site of a Forest Service work center. Next come White River Park and Murphy Flats in the vicinity of where the White River enters the South Fork. Salmon Forks is several river miles downstream from Murphy Flats. Here Big Salmon Creek, the outlet of Big Salmon Lake, enters the river. Farther downstream are Little Salmon Park and Black Bear Meadows. After Black Bear, the South Fork Canyon becomes much narrower, deeper and more heavily timbered.

Most of the tributary waters of the South Fork of the Flathead come in from the east slopes of the Swan Range. The best known of these streams, and the ones with trails leading in from the high country and the Swan Valley, are Hahn, Youngs and Gordon Creeks. They reach the Flathead drainage in the Danaher region. The White River comes in from the east farther downriver, as does Black Bear Creek. Where the river leaves the wilderness, Bunker Creek and the Spotted Bear River join the South Fork of the Flathead. Youngs and Hahn Creek drainages, with their many meadows, are very scenic in their lower reaches. Just a few miles below the start of the South Fork, Gordon Creek reaches the South Fork Valley. Gordon Pass is a major route into this region by way of the Holland Lake country and the Swan Range. Big Salmon Lake, just upstream from where Big Salmon Creek meets the South Fork, is a mountain gem. It's about four-and-a-half miles long and one-half mile wide, and sits 20 miles from Holland Lake in the Swan Valley and about another 20 miles from the Spotted Bear area.

There are many other less well known drainages and trails that offer scenic surprises. The Picture Ridge Trail is such a spot. It is on the west slopes above the South Fork and not very far from the Spotted Bear country. It reaches its highest elevation at 7,729' Picture Point. The trail starts at the Bunker Creek Road and comes out at the Black Bear Guard Station on the river. Get water whenever you have a chance when hiking this trail, especially late in the summer or fall.

There are several Forest Service back-country guard stations found throughout the South Fork of the Flathead, as well as in other parts of the Bob. These are, for the most part, simple cabins often hidden from view, that the Forest Service uses for administrative purposes, especially during the hunting season. They are not for public use. Occasionally you'll see the ruins of other cabins used by early-day trappers in the South Fork .

Bunker Creek is another major drainage reaching the South Fork, outside the wilderness. It has been described as "The Valley of the Moon without the aesthetics." A visit to this logged-over area will show you why.

As mentioned earlier, the South Fork is popular for floating. For the most part the waters are moderate, but there are some dangerous areas. Floaters often have outfitters or friends with horses pack their rafts to various points along the river. Floaters usually leave their cars at points to the south of Hungry Horse Reservoir. For those going all the way to the reservoir, a three-mile portage is required around an impassable gorge, near the mouth of Bunker Creek. For more information, the Forest Service puts out a special brochure on the three forks of the Flathead River. It contains vital information for floaters.

Top: Looking from the ridge above the White River into the South Fork of the White River in the Flathead Alps country. The photo was taken in July of 1927. U.S. Forest Service photo.

Bottom: Looking down Gibson Lake towards the prairie country and the lower Sun River Canyon. Gibson Lake and Dam are on the Sun River. Sawtooth Ridge is on the right. U.S. Forest Service photo.

At right, the North Fork of the Birch Creek country. Mount St. Nichlos in Glacier National Park is visible on the center horizon.

The Southern Mountains and Lincoln Back Country

This region covers the country from a line on the west from Montour Creek to Danaher Mountain, eastward to Rogers Pass and the Continental Divide. Its northern boundary is a divide that runs along the crest of the range from Danaher Mountain to the Falls Creek country on the Rocky Mountain Front.

It's a smaller area than others in the Bob but encompasses some beautiful wild country. Highway 200 through the Blackfoot Valley provides excellent access via many secondary and gravel roads. Starting on the west side, trails lead out of Montour Creek toward Camp Pass and several smaller lakes on the south side of the Dry Fork Flathead Divide. Camp Lake, Lake Otatsy and Canyon Lake are small mountain lakes in a forested setting. Another trail leads to the canyon of the North Fork of the Blackfoot River, and into the Scapegoat Wilderness.

Several mountain peaks in this western sector are worth climbing. Especially interesting are 8,351' Lake Mountain and 7,901' East Spread Mountain. Both afford panoramas of much of the Scapegoat Wilderness and the country to the south. Other roads and trails from this North Fork of the Blackfoot country lead into the Scapegoat via Meadow Lake and Meadow Creek. From here there are many routes to take. One good possibility would be to start in the North Fork of the Blackfoot Canyon, going by way of the North Fork Cabin, and then head southeast along the east fork of the Blackfoot, past the Meadow Lake trail to Parker-Webb and Hart Lakes. Side trails lead to the Continental Divide in the vicinity of Caribou Peak and Big Horn Lake. From Hart Lake you can walk the five miles out to the Copper Creek Campground. You can arrange to leave a car here for the ride back to Lincoln or take your chance on hitch-hiking.

The Lincoln back country out of the town of Lincoln is very accessible along the many logging and other gravel roads, and opens up recreational opportunities, both in summer and winter. Much of this country is getting to be a favorite destination of skiers in the higher reaches and snowmobilers in the lower valleys.

9,411' Red Mountain, the highest summit in the Bob Marshall Country, is easily reached from the Lincoln area via logging roads or by other trails from Hart Lake. 7,771' Silver King Mountain in the Alice Creek area near Lincoln is also readily reached. Roads go well into the valley of Alice Creek.

There are many facilities in the town of Lincoln, a mountain community that bills itself as a gateway to the wilderness.

For newcomers to wilderness and camping experiences, perhaps the Lincoln back country and the regions of the North Fork of the Blackfoot River offer excellent testing grounds for short journeys.

The Swan Range

The Swan Range provides a majestic western boundary for the Bob Marshall country. Certainly this range would have to be considered one of the most beautiful in Montana. Besides guarding the Bob Marshall Wilderness, it presides over the equally impressive and beautiful Swan Valley.

The crest of the range forms the western boundary of much of the Bob Marshall Wilderness. However, since this book is about the entire Bob Marshall *country,* the Swan Range is included because much of its west face is unroaded wild country deserving of wilderness status. Indeed, it is part of this entire eco-system. At the time of this writing, much of this area is being considered for inclusion in the wilderness system, and its chances for wilderness status appear good.

For purposes of defining the Swan Range as a region within the Bob Marshall country, we can consider it to run from 7,234' Columbia Mountain on the north, a peak just southeast of the town of Columbia Falls, for approximately 130 miles, to 8,062' Danaher Mountain and the start of the drainage of the South Fork of the Flathead. This distance is measured along the crest.

The northern 50 miles of the Swan Range crest are not within the wilderness area. Parts of it, especially the east slopes coming out of Hungry Horse Lake, are heavily roaded and logged. The west side, because of its steepness and unstable soils, has fewer roads. Trails run along the crest of the range out of Columbia Falls.

Approximately midway is an island of wild country, the Jewel Basin hiking area, and what a jewel it is. The Basin is accessible from the Echo Lake region in the Swan Valley or from the Hungry Horse Lake side. There are at least 28 beautiful lakes within these 15,349 acres of high mountain country. The Jewel Basin hiking area is a specially designated back-country use area. Elevations range from 7,530' Mount Aeneas, to a low point of 4,240' at Graves Creek. Here we have another example of low mountains with great relief. Special maps of the Jewel Basin area are available through the Forest Service.

From the southern end of Swan Lake, and from Swan Village, a trail heads to 7,406' Sixmile Mountain on the Swan divide. From here the trail follows the crest south to Inspiration Point and Pass, the border of the Bob Marshall Wilderness. Roads, visible on Forest Service maps, also lead to trails that eventually reach this divide route. Inspiration Pass is a major northern route into the northern sectors of the Bob Marshall Wilderness. From Inspiration Point south, the range becomes more spectacular and wilder. The canyons become very steep and narrow with raging torrents of water flowing through them in the spring. Just south of Inspiration Pass, 9,289' Swan Peak, one of the major sentinels of the Swan Range, rises. This is one of the few peaks in the Bob Marshall country holding active glaciers. These rivers of ice, found along the east and north sides of the peak, are kept alive by very heavy winter snows. Nestled far below Swan Peak is Sunburst Lake, a high cirque gem.

South of Swan Peak, Lion Creek Pass offers another major route into the Bob Marshall Country by way of Palisades and Little Salmon Creeks. The route up the Swan-face side goes through some beautiful stands of giant cedars. Farther down range, Smith Creek Pass is another route to the Swan summits, and eventually into the South Fork country. The trail joins up with the one coming over Lions Creek Pass to Little Salmon Creek.

Just west of Condon the second highest peak in the Bob Marshall country, 9,356' Holland Peak, reaches to the clouds. Holland Peak is considered by many people to be the most spectacular summit in the Swan Range. It sits amidst a jumble of other towering mountains, characterized by the two huge waterfalls emanating from the upper and lower Rumble Creek Lakes, just below its west face. The east side of this massif, like Swan Peak, features several active glaciers. Forest Service maps show more glaciers than actually exist. For instance, some are shown to be in Albino Basin, just to the north of Holland Peak, but they are probably no more than persistent snowfields that disappear some years. Holland Peak, like many others along the Swan Range, requires quite a physical effort to gain the top. The relief here ranges upwards to 5,500 feet, and much of it is straight up in a hurry. South of Holland Peak, and extending for many miles, are some beautiful basins holding many high cirque lakes. Routes leading into the Bob go through some of these areas. Holland Lake is a starting point for many of the trails as well as two of the major routes into the Bob Marshall country from the west. Sitting astride, or just below, the divide are bodies of water such as the Terrace Lakes, Woodward Lake, the Necklace Lakes, Pendant Lakes, Upper Holland Lake, Lick Lake, Koessler Lake, Doctor Lake and George Lake, to name a few. To the people of the Swan Valley this is the best country Montana has to offer.

The trails out of Holland Lake, favorites of horsepackers, are steep and get one into the back country in a hurry. The two major routes are over Gordon Pass from Upper Holland Lake and down Gordon Creek into the South Fork of the Flathead, or via the Pendant or Necklace Lakes to Big Salmon Creek and Big Salmon Lake below. The distances from Holland Lake deep into the back country are great and most people prefer to use horses. I have hiked across the Bob Marshall and prefer to take it from east to west, coming out at Holland Lake.

From the Seeley Lake area Pyramid Pass offers access to the upper reaches of the South Fork of the Flathead drainage. Trails from here lead to Youngs Creek. Other less-used passes are in the vicinity of Monture Mountain. Youngs Pass is another popular trail and also leads to Youngs Creek. Hahn Creek Pass, out of the Monture Creek country on the southern end of the range in the Blackfoot Valley, is another favorite horse route into the upper stretches of the South Fork country.

Because of the terrain, the eastern flanks of the Bob Marshall country offer more roaded access to the wilderness boundary than does the Swan side. However, there is ample roading in the lower reaches of the Swan Valley to enable motorized vehicle enthusiasts to get a closer look at some of the steep slopes and high peaks of the Swan Range. There are loop logging roads off of the Swan highway that rise to high ridge lines and open to excellent views. The Swan Range, then, just like the Rocky Mountain Front, offers something for everyone.

CHAPTER THREE

Weather

by Rick Graetz

The vastness of the Bob Marshall Country and its continental-divide spine dictate varied and unpredictable weather. One thing for certain though, the Bob experiences it all ... from 100 degrees above to 60 degrees below, from drought to floods, and from deep snow and roaring winds to total calm.

The Continental Divide serves as a continuous barrier that robs moisture from many of the storm systems crossing this wilderness country; hence most of the precipitation falls on the divide and west to the Swan Crest. The Swan Range itself is a formidable wall that takes its share of precipitation, so much so that there are small glaciers surviving on the north sides of several peaks.

It is possible to watch a storm in progress on the Continental Divide along the Chinese Wall from just a few miles to the east with no threat of getting wet. The stronger frontal systems minimize the mountain obstacles and can spread their moisture on both sides of the divide. These stronger systems have enough power and moisture in them to overcome the down-draft, drying-out effect as the moist air crosses the divide. The storms that don't make it over places like Scapegoat and the Chinese Wall simply dry out as the air that has just risen to cross the barrier starts warming on its descent to the east side of the mountains.

It is interesting to look at the sky from places like the North Fork of Birch Creek or the Teton Canyons, on the eastern fringes, and watch clouds flowing eastward grow smaller and disappear.

Thunderstorms of late spring and summer are usually spawned along the divide and the higher ranges. The air rises rapidly as it heats, and intense storms are created that move anywhere regardless of terrain.

Precipitation in the Bob as a whole is heaviest in the spring, especially May and June. Up in the higher peaks there is a more-even distribution throughout most of the year.

As mentioned, most of the snow or rain that falls on the Bob falls from the west to the divide. This is quite evident by the denser vegetation cover on the west side; the closer to the prairie country and Rocky Mountain Front, the sparser the growth. The strong winds on the east side dry out the country, taking moisture from the soil, further hindering growth.

Snow is also heaviest in the spring months; however, east of the divide, some of the deepest snowfall can occur during the coldest months of December, January and February. Actually snowstorms occuring during this time to the east of the divide can dump as much snow as any single storm west of the divide. The process that brings these storms to the Rocky Mountain Front region is known as upsloping. The systems come from the east and southeast, bringing up warm, moist Gulf of Mexico air that collides with the cold arctic air that often sits along the Front. Precipitation becomes quite intense owing to the abrupt uplifting of air. These storms can carry over into the rest of the Bob because the mountains to the west create more uplifting; however, the farther west, the lighter the snow.

This same procedure is often responsible for the drenching rain storms or early fall snows that the Bob Marshall east of the divide often experiences. These warm, moist storms heading toward the Bob from the southeast can cause the northerly winds that trail them to pull cold air from the north, further intensifying them and deepening the cold air mass.

The Rocky Mountain Front is known for its chinook winds, or snow-eaters as the Indians called them. These are warm, dry winds that can bring temporary respite from long periods of extreme cold. When they occur the temperature may rise from 30 degrees below zero to 30 degrees above within a couple of hours or less. There have been reports of a 26-degree rise in 45 seconds and 43 degrees in 15 minutes. Thirty inches of snow can disappear overnight.

The chinooks result from a steady, warm and moist westerly or southwesterly flow of air across Montana. This pattern also shows a high-pressure system to the south of the state over Nevada and Utah, and a low-pressure system to the north in Canada. As the moisture-laden winds begin to rise to cross the mountains of the Bob, they release their precipitation, usually in the form of heavy wet snow, on the uphill side. As they rapidly come down the mountain front, they become warmer and drier. At times their approach is heralded by a freight-train-like sound through the down-slope canyons.

The country east of the Chinese Wall and the other mountains of the Continental Divide also witnesses another extreme, that of severe cold, a result of arctic outbreaks. Temperatures may reach 40 to 60 degrees below zero. If the arctic air is deep enough, and comes on strong north winds, the cold air spills over to the valleys west of the divide, putting the entire wilderness complex in a dome of very cold air. The record low temperature for the contiguous 48 states was set on the southern edge of the Bob Marshall Country at Rogers Pass when the mercury dipped to 70 degrees below zero on January 20, 1954. Actually it was probably colder as the thermometer's minimum marking was 70 below, and that reading was observed at 2:00 a.m. The coldest temperature usually occurs just before sunrise.

Whereas chinooks occur in winter when the storm track moves into Canada, the arctic air is brought down by the storm trails moving far to the south of Montana. While the chinook winds cause rapid warming along the Rocky Mountain Front, the cold northern air has the opposite effect. At Browning, just east of the Front, the temperature once plummeted from a 44 degrees above zero to 56 degrees below zero in 24 hours.

The general weather pattern of the Bob Marshall Country is possible to describe if one keeps in mind that in some years there can be great fluctuations.

Summers are warm and dry with occasional thunderstorms. West of the divide the humidity is somewhat higher and these storms may occur with greater frequency. East of the divide the air is drier and often the temperatures are higher, with 90 to 100 degrees not uncommon. As summer turns to fall, some of the greatest temperature variations occur. Often it may be 40 degrees warmer in the afternoon than at first light. At this time of the year the sun is up long enough to heat the day, yet the nights are longer, and radiation cooling takes place.

In early September, usually a week or two of storminess prevails, with the mountain snowpack beginning to accumulate right after Labor Day in the higher elevations. After this interlude of stormy weather, a big high-pressure ridge usually builds over the west, and the Bob Marshall Country enjoys clear, dry air with warm days and cold nights through the early part of fall. Later, in October and early November, snowstorms can occur at any time. By November the snowpack is beginning to build in the valleys.

As the winter settles in, the storms, especially west of the divide, increase, and the colder air begins filling the lower elevations. November, December and January are stormy months in the Bob. East of the divide it is quite often very cold, although occasionally a chinook will break up the cold. When this arctic air from the east seeps through the canyons and over the mountains to the west side of the divide, the canyons and valleys experience strong ground blizzards as northerly winds are pushing the cold air into this section of the wilderness. Below-zero readings and a low wind chill are common. In February and early March, longer periods of clear, cold weather seem to be more prevalent, interrupted at times by a chinook. From late March through June, this country receives much of its annual precipitation. Snow is usually the dominant form of precipitation well into May, and then the heavier rains come.

The annual snowpack, in winter and spring, is quite variable and individual seasons can have as little as 50 percent of average to as high as 170 percent of the norm. Since about 70 percent of the spring and summer streamflow comes from winter snow, its accumulation has a marked effect on runoff.

In late April, the lower elevations and southfacing slopes begin to lose their snow cover, and the streams start to rise slowly. By mid-May, the lower areas are usually bare, and all areas with snowcover are showing considerable melting, swelling the streams to their maximum flows. As the snowline recedes, streams begin to drop and clear. However, the snow remains in the higher elevations into July, aiding the water supply of the stream systems. There are periods of clear skies during the spring and some years can be quite dry, but for the most part the weather is very unsettled this time of the year as the air is warming and holds more moisture.

Ray Mills of the Choteau district of the U.S. Forest Service measures the depth and water content on a snow course at Wrong Creek. U.S. Forest Service photo.

Snow Surveys

Because of its size, the Bob Marshall ecosystem is very important to the overall water supply of much of Montana. It is for this reason that there are about 30 snow courses throughout the wilderness and surrounding areas. These courses are measured from three to seven times each year, and the data gathered is used primarily for forecasting potential runoff during the spring and early summer.

Ray Mills of the Choteau Ranger Station, which takes in the Teton and Sun River Ranger Districts covering almost all of the Bob Marshall country east of the divide, has been measuring the snow-course sites in these areas since 1968. He primarily covers the courses in the Sun River drainage. They are located at Cabin Creek, Wrong Creek, Wrong Ridge and

Goat Mountain. The route he covers is about 76 miles and takes 6 to 8 days to complete, depending upon the snow conditions. As this is wilderness, his travel is by snowshoes or skis, and he prefers to use snowshoes. He has seen the all-time high snow measurement in this area, as well as the all-time low. In 1972 Ray measured 94.4 inches of snow on March 1 at Wrong Ridge and 29 inches of water content. On March 1, 1981 at the same site, he measured only 33.2 inches of snow and 9.9 inches of water. Normal water content for March 1 is 18.3 inches and about 60 inches of snow.

The actual measurements are taken by a two-inch diameter aluminum pipe in three-foot sections that screw together. The snow depth is recorded when the cutter on the pipe comes in contact with the ground. The pipe and snow core within the pipe are carefully lifted out of the snow and then weighed. Subtracting the weight of the empty tube from the combined weight of the tube and snow core gives the water content in inches. A graph of snow depth and water content shows the percent of water or density in the snowpack, which varies greatly from year to year and even from month to month. The course measurements in this Sun River country are taken three times a year.

The following is a chart showing the various snow courses in or near the Bob Marshall Wilderness. The measurements shown were taken on April 1. The deeper snow readings are from sites west of the divide. For instance, Camp Misery and Noisy Basin are in the Swan Range to the west of Hungry Horse Lake. Mt. Lockhart is at Teton Pass ski area in the Rocky Mountain Front country.

The actual average snowfall in the Bob Marshall Wilderness, in the higher elevations, ranges from 300 to 500 inches a year. Some sites get more and others get quite a bit less.

Snow Courses in/near Bob Marshall Wilderness

Snow Course	Elevation Feet	Start of Record	Normal Apr. 1 Depth Inches	Max Measured Depth Inches	Year of Max Depth	1963-77 Average Apr. 1 SWE Inches
Badger Pass	6900	1964	99	150	1972	41.7
Beaver Lake	5900	1964	65	101	1972	25.8
Big Creek	6750	1941	112	155	1972	47.6
Blue Lake	5900	1969	70	104	1972	46.3
Cabin Creek	5200	1949	25	41	1954	7.2
Camp Misery	6400	1962	127	180	1975	52.0
Copper Bottom	5200	1971	34	63	1972	11.9
Copper Camp	6950	1971	86	139	1972	34.2
Copper Creek	5700	1962	47	79	1972	16.1
Copper Lake Creek	6100	1971	73	107	1972	26.3
Coyote Hill	4200	1947	36	51	1950	10.7
Desert Mountain	5600	1937	52	70	1950	17.3
Emery Creek	4350	1976	51	55	1978	17.1
Fatty Creek	5500	1962	68	89	1978	25.1
Five Bull	5700	1948	26	46	1971	7.6
Freight Creek	6000	1948	52	81	1972	17.2
Goat Mountain	7000	1934	40	58	1956	11.6
Gunsight Lake	6300	1964	101	140	1972	42.7
Holbrook	4530	1951	35	53	1972	10.7
Marias Pass	5250	1934	57	94	1954	19.2
Mt. Lockhart	6400	1969	68	94	1972	23.9
Noisy Basin	6040	1974	118	161	1974	48.3
North Fork Jocko	6330	1941	120	152	1967 & 1972	48.4
Spotted Bear Mountain	7000	1948	50	72	1948	16.3
Trinkus Lake	6100	1949	111	147	1959	46.3
Twin Creeks	3580	1951	39	64	1972	12.1
Upper Holland Lake	6200	1948	97	135	1971	38.6
Waldron	5600	1969	37	52	1972	11.1
Wrong Creek	5700	1949	47	73	1954 & 1972	15.4
Wrong Ridge	6800	1949	60	94	1972	21.5

Source: Soil Conservation Service Snow Surveys, Bozeman, MT

CHAPTER FOUR

Wildlife

by Bob Cooney

I have had the good fortune of being closely associated with the wildlife of the Bob Marshall since the early 1930s. For several years with the Forest Service, I gathered information on the elk herds and other game animals of that area, and spent nearly 30 years with the Montana Fish and Game Department in game management. Throughout that time the department put an emphasis on wildlife in wilderness, including the Bob Marshall. Since retirement I've made many hiking and horseback trips to the back country.

The material in this chapter has been gained through personal observations over many years and from the findings of others especially knowledgeable of the area.

The presentation is not formal. I have thought of it much as though we were visiting around a campfire back in those remote mountains.

Deer in velvet. Tom Ulrich photo.

Mammals

Since elk have played such an important role in the wildlife picture of the entire area, it might be well to begin with them.

This is truly elk country. There are several major herds identified by their home ranges. These are the Sun River, the South Fork of the Flathead, and the Middle Fork of the Flathead herds. Another fairly large group summers in the upper North Fork of the Blackfoot River drainage. Other scattered bands are found around the edge of this vast area.

Because they are wild and shy, we may not see many elk, but we will constantly see evidence of their presence.

A network of elk trails crisscrosses the area. Some lead to favorite feeding and resting places, others to heavily frequented natural licks. Well worn migration trails cross high divides.

Heavily scarred little pines, here and there, indicate the early fall activity of bull elk in cleaning and polishing their antlers for the rutting season. Small mud wallows also can be found in these same areas as further evidence of bulls' activities in the fall.

Winter ranges are the most critical to the life of the elk. It is possible to recognize these important places even during summer visits. Favored shrubs, such as willows, often show the results of heavy browsing. Nearby lodgepole pine thickets bear evidence of high-lining where wintering elk have resorted to eating the needles as high as they could reach when more favored food was not available. Scars appear on aspen boles where elk have scraped off bits of bark as winter food. And the ever-present, weather-resistant, compact droppings indicate elk have wintered there.

The presence of newborn calves enhances the loveliness of spring time in these mountains. The cows select calving grounds with care. Usually they are along the migration routes from winter to higher summer ranges. They must be below the receding snow line of late May and early June. In such places lush plant growth assures a plentiful milk supply.

The newly born spotted calves are difficult to see lying motionless among low, shrubby plants, often along the edge of an aspen grove. Of course the cows are very protective; they seem to have little difficulty in chasing away coyotes, but bears occasionally present a more serious problem. In such cases a number of cows will sometimes join together in an attempt to discourage the intruder.

With the coming of summer, cows and calves move up toward the heads of drainages. In doing so they sometimes have to cross fairly large streams and rivers. They are strong, proficient swimmers.

Cow and calf groups often summer in high partially wooded basins. If they are disturbed, the anxious calling of both the cows and calves creates a compelling sound that must aid in keeping them together as they move through the woods.

The bulls generally spend the summers in somewhat the same areas but stay pretty much by themselves. Their leisurely days are spent feeding, resting and growing new antlers.

Elk tend to move to slightly lower areas with the coming of early fall and the rutting season. This is a time of great activity among the bulls. They use large amounts of energy in attempting to collect and hold groups of cows and calves, called harems. The thrilling, high-pitched bugling of the bulls rings out across wooded canyons, even throughout the nights.

There seems to be more bluffing and sparring than actual fighting, but the bulls do get serious at times. A long-time friend of mine, Paul Hazel, who spent nearly 60 years in the Bob Marshall Country, was close to one of these battles near Beartop Lookout. He heard elk bugling in the timber below him. When he arrived on the scene he found evidence of a terrific struggle. The ground was torn up, and a considerable amount of elk hair was scattered about. He was startled to find an antler that had been broken from the head of one of the bulls.

I often think of the striking view of a bull elk and his large harem up near the head of Baldy Bear Creek on the North Fork of the Sun River. On a cross-country hike following game trails in the early fall, I came through the edge of some timber and above me not far away on an open beargrass slope were elk. Some 20 cows and calves were lying down in a fairly compact group. Just above them stood a magnificent bull. There was a sheer escarpment of the Continental Divide in the background. The sky was blue with a few drifting clouds. As I fumbled to get my camera ready a little breeze shifted from me to the elk and suddenly a once-in-a-lifetime picture was gone.

The elk herds in the Bob Marshall Wilderness Country have interesting histories. All have developed from small native groups that were back in these mountains around the turn of the century.

In its development, the Sun River elk herd faced especially difficult problems. Unlike the others, this herd in the early years had to compete with large numbers of cattle well back in the forest. In spite of this, there was a steady increase among the elk. By the mid-'20s, numbers had risen to a point where elk began to drift out onto private lands along the foothills during the winter months.

The Sun River Game Preserve established by the Montana Legislature in 1912 is an outgrowth of early concern for the preservation and development of elk. This area of approximately 200,000 acres lies west from the North and South Forks of the Sun River to the Continental Divide. It is presently looked upon with mixed feelings. Some maintain that, although it may have had beneficial effects on the early growth of the elk herd, it now presents problems in regard to gaining better elk distribution and a more orderly harvest. Others feel it still possesses value as a wildlife sanctuary.

Even with the removal of all cattle from the upper Sun River ranges in the early '30s, elk continued to drift to private lands outside the mountains. It became such a problem that the Department of Fish and Game assigned a pioneer warden, the late Bruce Neal, to devise ways of herding elk back into the deep-snow country of the forest and holding them there. He conducted this difficult task for some 17 winters. I had a first-hand look at the work in helping Bruce with the herding a number of times. Sportsmen and ranchers also aided in this difficult task.

There were countless snowshoe and horseback miles of herding during all those years. Occasionally about a thousand elk were moved at a time. They were pushed back along steep and snow-packed migration trails. Even with all this effort, the program was not a solution. The underlying problem remained a lack of winter range to support this major herd.

Other related problems were becoming increasingly evident. The large bands of elk being pushed and held back in the mountains were competing seriously with bighorn sheep. Heavy winter losses took place among the bighorns, especially along the Sun River Canyon. Additional bits of available winter range above the Canyon on both forks of the Sun River were being overused by elk.

The future for the Sun River elk herd looked very bleak by the mid-'40s. It seemed inevitable that elk numbers would have to be drastically reduced, probably to a point where they would lose identity as a nationally recognized herd.

A break came in 1948. Two large adjoining ranch holdings in the foothills became available for purchase. It was the very grass and rolling timberlands the elk had been trying to reach during all those winters. As wonderful as it appeared for the elk, the Fish and Game Department found it would be impossible to act fast enough to meet the very short deadline specified by the sellers. Out-of-state money also was ready to make the purchase.

It looked as though this chance of a lifetime to save the Sun River elk herd was slipping away. At that critical point Tom Messelt, a sportsman from Great Falls, and Carl Malone, a rancher from Choteau, got together and made the necessary down payments. They held the land until the slower acquisition process by the State could be completed.

This beautiful foothill range, acquired just south of the Sun River and east of the massive Sawtooth Mountain, west of Augusta, was ideal to meet the winter needs of the long beleaguered elk herd. It possessed a desirable balance between rolling grasslands for feeding and timber stands as necessary sanctuary and shelter from storms.

Soon after the range was acquired by the state Fish and Game Department, it was visited by the late Dr. Olaus Murie, an internationally recognized wildlife authority, who called it one of the very finest winter elk ranges on the Continent. The 20,000-acre range was quickly made ready for winter use by elk, and they lost no time in reaching it. The major problem facing the elk herd had been solved.

Elk moved quickly through the bighorn sheep winter range along the Sun River canyon. The bighorns that had suffered so much from competition with elk began a steady increase in numbers. The long-standing winter problem of elk on private lands along the foothills also greatly improved. Bruce Neal, who for all those winters had to push the elk that he loved back into the deep snow, was made the first manager of the game range. It is easy to imagine that for him it was a dream come true.

Work on the game range is continuous. Frequent horseback and snowshoe patrols are conducted and occasionally a helicopter makes passes during winter months to move outlying groups of elk onto the range. Many miles of boundary fence had to be constructed. The fence was specially designed with jacks and barbed wire with a jumping rail along the top. The rail was necessary so elk could gauge their jumps in moving on and off the range. It is stockproof, but the elk have no problem jumping it.

In the summer and fall there is fire patrol as a grassfire could be disastrous to the winter forage supply for the elk. The manager is available for field trips over the range by school children and others from surrounding communities. He also helps with the wildlife work being conducted on the range and back in the wilderness beyond. Recreational visitors drop in throughout the year. In the winter the manager can suggest the best views of the elk without disturbing them.

There have been short hunting seasons on the range in the fall before major numbers of migrating elk move on. Some of the elk tend to linger on the winter range year-round; and a fall harvest of these animals ensures as much grass as possible will be available for the critical winter period.

Bert Goodman, who had the privilege of working with Bruce Neal on the game range a long time ago, is the present manager.

In more recent years the Montana Department of Fish, Wildlife and Parks and The Nature Conservancy have acquired additional winter range areas north of the Sun River. These important foothill and swamp lands lie north and south of the Teton Canyon, along the Rocky Mountain Front. They provide important winter foraging areas for elk and deer as well as highly valuable habitat for grizzly bears.

The Sun River elk herd, which has gone through such difficult times, faces a bright future unless seriously disrupted by oil and gas exploration and development on the vital winter ranges or along the elk's major migration routes.

The South and Middle Forks of the Flathead elk herds have been quite similar in their development. From the standpoint of the elk, both benefited from extensive forest fires that swept through these mountain areas in the early part of this century. Willow, serviceberry, mountain maple and other browse (brushy plants) soon sprung up throughout the burned-over areas. Snow gets quite deep in both of these big drainages. As the brush plants stood up well in the snow, they became a very important part of the winter food supply for steadily increasing numbers of elk.

The situation began to change as the years went by. Slower growing lodgepole pine appeared in dense stands throughout these old burns. The pines gradually crowded and shaded out many of the browse plants. This reduced the amount of winter forage available to the elk. Quite heavy losses have been experienced, particularly during severe winters.

A recent Forest Service policy of letting certain natural fires burn, may allow wild fire to again assume something of its historic role in plant succession and might allow an increase in elk forage plants.

Mule and white-tailed deer frequent many areas in the Bob Marshall Wilderness Country. The mule deer prefer the rougher terrain. In contrast the white-tails are often found in timber and brushy meadows along stream and river bottoms.

Both often make lengthy treks to and from their winter ranges. Recent findings have indicated a portion of the mule deer that winter along the eastern edge of the Rocky Mountain Front drift long distances to the west into the very heart of the Bob Marshall Wilderness to spend the summers.

Both species prefer leaves, buds and twigs of browse plants and even juniper and fir needles for winter feed. At least on the eastern side of the Continental Divide, their choice of diet differs considerably from the grass so favored by elk and bighorn sheep.

The unique, stiff-legged, bouncing gait of running mule deer makes them look as though they are going up and down about as much as forward, but this method of travel is well adapted to the rocky, rough country where they live. Sometimes, however, this gait has its disadvantages. For example along the Sun River Canyon in the winter, coyotes occasionally chase mule deer out onto the ice of Gibson Lake. Tracks show that the deer, so sure footed on rough hillsides, are badly handicapped when running on ice.

Deer often come into summer camps in the daylight back in the mountains. They seem salt hungry and will lick or chew anything salty. Horseback riders have found it best to hang up their gear or cover it with canvas. Sweaty bits of leather such as cinches can be damaged by deer chewing on them during the night.

A friend of mine in camp up near the Continental Divide had placed his saddle near his tent for the night. At daylight he was startled to see his bridle go scooting by the open tent flap. He looked out and was just in time to see a mule deer doe departing across the meadow with one of the reins in her mouth.

It is always a thrill to have a white-tailed deer that has been hiding till you almost pass by bound away with those great arching leaps and its beautiful tail "flagging."

Bighorn sheep are found for the most part on the eastern side of the Bob Marshall Country. They often move some distance from high summer ranges to winter along south-facing rocky slopes that are interspersed with patches of grass.

The bighorns have gone through some difficult times. From the '20s to the '40s the bighorns and large numbers of elk were competing for a limited winter food supply. Since the elk were more numerous and are more aggressive feeders, bighorns suffered considerably. Heavy winter losses first became apparent among the sheep in the mid-'20s with the build up of elk. Losses continued periodically until the purchase of the elk winter range in the foothills in 1948. Since that time elk have migrated quickly through the critical mountain sheep ranges, no longer creating a problem. The bighorns have increased until they are now one of the finest groups of this relatively rare animal in the United States.

Big rams with their massive curled horns spend much of their time in high rocky places apart from the ewes, lambs and young rams. Many drift well north along the high crest of the Rocky Mountain Front Range. Almost overnight they appear among the ewes with the onset of the mating season in the late fall. This is an exciting time to watch the struggles for supremacy among the rams and to hear the sharp crack of horns slamming together in bouts between these powerful and blocky-built combatants.

With the end of the mating season many of the rams appear to patch up their differences as they move off in small groups.

A number of newly developing herds of bighorns in Montana have been started by animals captured in the Sun River Canyon area.

Mountain goats are a breed apart. Their wide range of food selection, heavy cold-resistant coats and superb mountaineering ability make it possible for them to live year round in a high, harsh environment. They are found singly or in small scattered groups along the mountain crests of much of the Bob Marshall Wilderness Country.

Because of the goats' apparent dislike of becoming rain soaked, their home ranges are often in convenient proximity to overhanging cliff faces or shallow caves where they can remain dry. Only if you are lucky or persistent will you catch a glimpse of moving white specks threading their way along narrow ledges on high percipitous cliffs.

Their dagger-sharp, curving horns are truly formidable weapons. A lightning-fast thrust of the head can inflict destructive damage. It is no wonder they have gained the respect of even the larger predators that occasionally frequent their alpine homeland. The little kids, born around the first of June, stay close to their mothers but can soon perform surprising feats of rock climbing. If a golden eagle should soar near, the little fellows frequently take a position directly beneath their mothers, and those who study the goat believe that eagles do not present a very serious threat to the kids.

Mountain goats have been captured in several places in the Bob Marshall area and successfully transplanted into new ranges in the state.

As far as we know moose have not been abundant in the Bob Marshall area. These big fellows are presently found rather thinly scattered in willow thickets and adjoining timber lands along the Middle Fork of the Flathead and its side drainages. They are widely dispersed in the lower South Fork of the Flathead drainage and farther up river in the Youngs Creek-Danaher area. Moose occasionally are seen in the Gates Park region along the North Fork of the Sun River on the east side of the Divide. Their long legs make it possible for them to winter in areas where snow becomes quite deep.

The grizzly bear or silvertip is surely the animal that best typifies the true wild character of the wilderness. Just to see its great claw-tipped tracks in some muddy place along a mountain trail is an unforgettable thrill. That they are here at all is due to the retention of a few large undisturbed mountain strongholds where these huge, but relatively shy, animals can survive. Human activities have eliminated them from almost all of their former range throughout the West, south of the Canadian border.

Glacier Park and adjoining areas and the Bob Marshall Wilderness Country make up the very core of the vital Northern Continental Divide Grizzly Range. All of the requirements of this big bear are found there, especially a spacious, generally undisturbed environment.

The grizzlies have been classified as omnivorous. They subsist on a wide variety of food material, both plant and animal.

They usually leave their winter dens in late March or early April. Some of the females would have given birth to cubs in their dens during mid-winter. They then move to lower elevations to feed upon grasses and forbs (weed-like plants). They also seek out the remains of any animals that died during the winter.

With the coming of summer many of the bears work their way to higher elevations where they dig and consume tubers, fleshy roots and bulbs. They are well equipped with their long claws for this type of foraging. In their constant search for food, many rocks are turned over and stumps and rotten logs torn apart to obtain insects and larvae. Later in the summer they usually turn their attention to ripening berries. Huckleberries are most favored.

Where whitebark pine stands are available, at about 6,000 feet and above, the grizzlies search for nuts in the early fall. They often dig out squirrel caches to obtain this rich source of food.

Field work by the Craighead brothers and others has documented that the big bears often have their winter dens dug and ready for occupancy by mid-fall. However, they apparently wait to go into them until a heavy snowstorm is in progress, perhaps in late November or early December. In that way, they leave no tell-tale tracks leading to their dens.

The future of the grizzly is troubled and it has been classified as a threatened wildlife species. This assures special consideration to the bear and to the critical wilderness habitat upon which its survival depends.

During the Montana legislative session of 1983 the grizzly was designated the Montana State Animal.

The black bear with its several color phases of brown has somehow managed to avoid the threats to its existence that have plagued its big cousin, the grizzly. It is found roaming in fair numbers throughout much of the Bob Marshall area. Its home range seems often to include areas a bit lower in elevation than the grizzly. The black bear's food consists of a wide variety of plant and animal materials.

Because the black bear has adjusted fairly well to man's activities, its future is not as closely tied to the preservation of wilderness as has been so clearly demonstrated with the grizzly.

The gray wolf in the Bob Marshall Country ekes out a precarious existence apparently as an occasional visitor from Canada. It has been classified as an endangered species. The Glacier Park area and Bob Marshall wilderness country is a corridor of relatively undisturbed mountains that might have some potential as a link with the wolf populations in Canada to the north.

A glimpse of a wolf, or even the faint sound of one howl, back in some remote place would be a tremendous thrill. I know because I heard one once, a long time ago up near the headwaters of the North Fork of the Sun River.

Coyotes and their tracks, as well as their droppings here and there along mountain trails, tell us these adaptable yet wary animals are very much a part of the wilderness.

To be awakened with the first light of morning by their wild barking cries in the distance seems an especially fitting way to start the day.

Their choice of food is varied. Mice, ground squirrels, birds, rabbits, and bits of carrion along with some plant material, are important items of their diet. If snow is deep and crusted, so deer break through while coyotes can run on top, weak animals are sometimes taken. On rare occasions, as we mentioned earlier, coyotes catch deer on a frozen lake and can prey easily on them there.

The red fox is sometimes seen in these mountains.

The mountain lion or cougar, in Montana, has been classified as a game animal and is protected by quite restrictive regulations. Although a portion of the lion's requirements are satisfied by capturing smaller animals, deer and sometimes elk appear to make up the staple food of these big cats. They are found rather thinly dispersed throughout the Bob.

The Canada lynx is found in remote places throughout the Bob Marshall area. This stealthy animal is truly a creature of remote places. It lives out its life back in wooded areas where snowfall is heavy. Its large fur-covered paws allow it to travel swiftly over the snow. The snowshoe hare is believed to be its most important prey, and the lynx numbers are closely tied to the population cycles of the hare.

The Canada lynx once was heavily trapped for its beautiful soft pelt. It has been classified as a fur-bearing animal and carefully protected. As they are especially wary and do much of their hunting at night, it would be an exceptional stroke of luck to see one. Just to know they are there is pleasure enough for most lovers of wildlife.

The smaller bobcat prefers for the most part the rough foothills and brushy canyon bottoms of the Rocky Mountain Front Range and other areas around the outer portion of the wilderness. There they search for cottontail rabbits and other small prey. They have been trapped quite heavily, but like the Canada lynx, have received increased protection since being placed on the fur-bearing animal list. In the fur trade, the spots along the lower portions of their body might have placed them in demand among the spotted cats of the world for which there is increasing concern.

The beaver attracted the first explorer-trappers into this part of the west a century and a half ago.

Gnawed aspen stumps, ponds, dams, lodges and food caches throughout river and stream bottoms are constant reminders of the presence of these energetic animals. Their lives are inseparably bound to water. Superb swimmers, they are rather slow on land where they are easy prey to a variety of the larger predators. Their ponds are keys to their survival. The bark of quaking aspen and willows make up much of their diet in these mountains. When they have cut down the trees near the ponds, the beavers become creatures of high risk. They have to travel longer distances from the safety of water to obtain their food. At some point they find it essential to leave their home ponds and move on to construct new ones nearer an adequate food supply.

The beaver of the Bob Marshall and other mountain ranges have the unique ability to sometimes alter the landscape. Many meadows along mountain drainages may well have once been narrow and relatively steep stream beds. Meadowlands and gently meandering streams were created where beaver ponds had been made, abandoned and filled with silt, then made again.

It is quite possible that the beautiful meadows of the Danaher Basin, near the headwaters of the South Fork of the Flathead, had their origin through centuries of beaver activity.

The river otter is the aquatic acrobat and clown of the weasel family. If we could follow their tracks in deep snow along one of the partially frozen rivers of the wilderness, they would reveal a series of jumps and then a long trench in the snow in which otters slide as far as they can. Then some more jumps and another slide continuing until they take us to an opening in the ice where otters swim and play. There might be scales, bits of fish and crayfish here and there near these openings in the river ice. The otter can reach high speeds through the water as it searches for elusive prey. These agile swimmers and comical overland travelers are found here and there along the rivers of our wilderness region.

The river banks of these same water courses are homeland for the otter's small cousin, the mink.

Wilderness fishermen are sometimes surprised to discover that the trout they momentarily left unattended along a river or streambank may well have disappeared by the time they returned. A hungry mink was quite possibly the culprit. As with all of the weasel tribe, they are voracious eaters, living on a variety of small animals, birds, crayfishes and fishes. In their search for food, this elegant member of the weasel family depends upon its ability as a good swimmer and climber.

The pine marten, sometimes called the American sable, is perfectly equipped for a life in mature timber stands. It prefers deep snow country where its fur-covered paws enable it to bound rapidly over soft fluffy snow. Marten are able to run down even the fleet snowshoe hares. At a moment's notice they are able to switch their hunting to the treetops, where they frequently capture pine squirrels. Here in the wilderness they are usually found in areas associated with mature spruce and alpine fir stands.

The marten has been trapped through the years for its soft, lustrous fur. It takes a hardy sort of woodsman to run a trapline during mid-winter in the deep snow country.

The fisher is a close relative of the pine marten. It is considerably larger in size and darker in color. The frosty sheen of its beautiful pelt made it highly prized in the fur trade.

For many years the fisher had apparently been gone from the mountain ranges of Montana. It was reintroduced in the late 1950s from British Columbia in a joint venture between the Department of Fish and Game and Forest Service. Sightings have been made along the heavily timbered west side of the South Fork of the Flathead, within the Bob Marshall Wilderness.

Fishers are known for their speed through the treetops. As the marten can catch the pine squirrel, the fisher is said to be able to out-climb the marten.

Its most unique prey is the plodding, but dangerously armed porcupine. The fisher has developed a lightning-like attack apparently from the front to avoid the potentially lethal quills. Foresters have been interested in the reintroduction of the fisher as it might reduce damage to pine trees by holding down the numbers of the bark gnawing porcupines, thus restoring a historic balance.

Badgers are sometimes seen along the more open portions of the intermountain valleys of the Bob Marshall area, where they do a great deal of digging in search of ground squirrels and other rodents. I remember an interesting little drama being played out between a badger and a coyote one spring sometime ago.

In watching a mountain meadow in the wilderness, I noticed a badger moving along, apparently hunting for ground squirrels. It was being rather closely followed by a coyote.

The badger started to dig, attempting to capture a meal. The coyote quickly trotted up and began watching nearby burrows in case the badger's activity might chase out a ground squirrel. After a time, the badger backed out from his excavation, apparently unsuccessful that time. The last I saw of this unlikely pair, the low slung badger was moving on, searching for another digging opportunity. The opportunistic coyote was tagging along.

The wolverine must be the most striking of the weasel tribe. This legendary animal is unexcelled in strength by any creature its size. The huge weasel is somewhat bear-like in shape and can weigh about 40 pounds.

It was thought the wolverine was gone from much of its historic range in Montana. Some time ago it began to reappear along the Continental Divide corridor out of Canada, through the Glacier Park area and down into the Bob Marshall Wilderness Country. These mostly solitary animals travel great distances in their constant search for food.

It has been especially pleasing to observe tracks of the wolverine on recent winter trips into the Bob Marshall. Even though they are back, they are seldom seen.

A friend of mine was watching the east face of the Chinese Wall for mountain goats a few summers ago when he was surprised to see two dark objects moving about among the rock slides at the base of the wall. With his binoculars he was able to make out wolverines. He thought they were probably a male and female traveling together during the brief mating season. They appeared to be searching for marmots.

The weasel or ermine is sometimes seen darting here and there in the wilderness. This veritable streak of brown becomes snow white except for its black tipped tail during the winter months. Mice and other small prey make up the food supply of this curious and agile little predator.

The red or pine squirrel is a good example of the area's many non-game species. They act like self-appointed sentinels. Their boisterous chattering often follows as we move through these otherwise quiet woods. We mentioned their inadvertant aid to the grizzly bear in storing away caches of nuts among the stands of whitebark pines. Digging out the nuts and feasting on them must be a great discovery for the big bear, but it can seriously deplete the squirrel's winter food supply.

Columbia ground squirrels and their burrows are often evident in the Bob Marshall. They are seen throughout open grassy parks and meadowlands on both sides of the Continental Divide. The plump little fellows are very alert as many of the meat-eating animals and birds search for them. They make an interesting chirping sound apparently as a warning signal.

Evidences of a small, secretive rodent are often found throughout mountain meadows of the Bob Marshall Wilderness Country in the form of mounds of earth freshly pushed up from an elaborate system of subterranean tunnels. The seldom-seen animal is the northern pocket gopher.

They are well equipped for their underground existence. External cheek pouches are used to transport food throughout their tunnels. These small rodents have especially well developed forearms with long sharp claws. These and their strong gnawing teeth make them ideally prepared for a lifetime of prodigious digging.

Underground plant parts such as roots and bulbs are their primary food. They are active the year round. With the melting of the snow, serpentine patterns of soil casts on the surface of the ground are unique reminders of their winter activities.

Although the slow moving porcupines are not seen very often, evidence of their feeding is obvious among many of the pine stands. They chew off patches of bark, especially during the wintertime.

The hoary or whistling marmot is well adapted to its remote homeland among rock slides and alpine meadows. It is sometimes seen and heard on the talus slopes along the base of the Chinese Wall and other high rocky areas of the Bob Marshall Wilderness country.

Their piercing whistle carries for long distances. It must serve as a very effective warning of golden eagles that glide into view along the precipitous cliffs above them. Their burrows are ordinarily under a jumble of large rocks that protect them from most predators.

The delightful little pika is another resident of the rock slides at higher elevations. These active little fellows have short rounded ears, soft rabbit-like fur and no visable tail.

They have a surprising number of names, among which are cony, rock rabbit, little chief hare and haymaker. The last refers to their interesting habit of collecting and curing various plants as a winter food supply. During the summer they dash out to the edge of the rock slides. Here they nip off green bits of grass and weeds. These are brought back to a convenient and sunny place among the rocks to cure. Dried plants from these small hay stacks are relished as food throughout the long harsh winters. These hardy little animals do not hibernate but remain active in their snug homes beneath the rock slides and deep snow of the high country.

The diminutive pikas blend well with the rocks where they live. A chirping call is usually the first evidence of their presence, but like the ventriloquist they do not appear to be where you heard the sound.

Birds

Birds, from the tiny kinglet to the majestic golden eagle, are a beautiful and vibrant part of the vast wildlife community of the Bob Marshall country. Some spend only the summers. Others are there throughout the year. Some, like the thrushes, are shy. In contrast the gray jays are often quite tame.

There is something very special about the sight of golden or mountain eagles soaring among the high peaks. They surely typify the feeling of freedom and spaciousness of these remote places.

Close glimpses of these large birds are rare and memorable. During a pleasant winter day three of us were hiking along a little game trail in the Rocky Mountain Front Range. We glanced up, and just above the tree tops came an eagle. As it passed overhead the late afternoon sun highlighted a glint of gold on the feathers at the nape of its neck. Just as quickly it was gone.

I have another fond memory, this one of the rare and endangered peregrine falcon. A number of years ago I left camp before daylight to be up at the base of the Chinese Wall when the first sunlight would touch it with a pinkish glow. A medium sized hawklike bird left a crevice among the rocks and flew almost directly over me. It had noticably pointed, swept-back wings and a shallow beat. Most exciting of all were the dark facial markings of the peregrine falcon. It is not known whether any of these rare birds still nest in the Bob Marshall Country.

Three of the grouse that inhabit this wilderness are quite frequently seen. They are the blue, the ruffed and the spruce grouse. The fourth is rare, found only by those who explore remote high places at timber line or above. It is the white tailed ptarmigan, a beautiful small grouse, perhaps left over from glacial times.

I still remember the first ptarmigan I saw. It was a day in early summer on the crest of Prairie Reef, well above timber line. I had a movie camera and tripod in my back pack. A pair of ptarmigan were picking away at some alpine plants nearby. Hastily I put on a telephoto lens and was attaching the camera to the tripod. When I finally took my eyes off the equipment and glanced at the birds, they were nearly under the tripod, too near for the telephoto. These beautiful little grouse were in their mottled summer plumage, and blended with the alpine tundra surroundings.

That winter I was able to scramble up on the Continental Divide at the head of Lick Creek on the North Fork of the Sun River. It was so icy I decided to leave my camera behind. From the top I was treated to a view of veritable sea of white peaks in all directions. What a chance for pictures. Then I began looking at a little object on a large windblown snowbank nearby. It turned out to be a ptarmigan, and this time, except for its dark eyes and bill it was as white as the snow itself.

These beautiful little fellows are thinly scattered along the mountain crests of the Continental Divide and adjacent ranges in the Bob Marshall Country. They are well adapted to the harsh environment in which they live, year round. They have feathers over the nostrils. There are also feathers on their legs and feet. The long, hairlike feathers on their feet enable them to walk easily on soft snow.

The spruce grouse or Franklin's is often called fool hen because of its gentleness. These small grouse sometimes frequent trails in the deep woods where they live. They may be seeking dusting opportunities. Hens and their chicks sometimes can be seen along these trails. The mothers are very protective. On the trail I occasionally used to make a squeaking sound like a chick. The little spruce grouse hens would invariably fluff up and come toward me. I have often thought they couldn't be that tame around a coyote or lynx. Like other grouse, their numbers fluctuate in a somewhat cyclic fashion through the years.

The larger blue grouse are quite wary. The hens nest at rather low elevations along river and creek bottom areas throughout much of the Bob Marshall Wilderness Country. With their chicks they move up the slopes as the insects and berries develop. By early fall they form flocks along the ridge tops where they frequently winter. During storm periods they sometimes tunnel into soft snow banks to spend the nights.

The ruffed grouse are usually found in the vicinity of brushy canyon and river bottoms. Their drumming sound is a pleasant harbinger to the coming of spring.

Waterfowl are not especially abundant in this wilderness region. A female common merganser with her string of little ones is always fun to watch as they paddle their way up one of the mountain rivers. It is surprising how fast the young can follow their mother if disturbed. By using their feet and stubby little wings they can scuttle quickly along the surface of the water.

The shy and uncommon harlequin ducks prefer fast moving waters along the upper reaches of the cold mountain rivers on both sides of the Continental Divide. The male is a splendid sight with striking white markings on a slate blue and rusty reddish background. They are sea ducks that come in from coastal waters to nest and raise their young.

Mallards, golden eyes, teals and others are seen on small meandering streams, beaver ponds and mountain lakes. Common loons visit Big Salmon Lake. Their wild cry is another of the lovely sounds of that remote area.

It is always pleasant to hear the hooting of a great horned owl in the quiet of a wilderness night. Among other owls of interest are the pygmy, barred, saw-whet and now and then the rare great gray owl.

The pileated woodpecker, almost the size of a crow, is surely a bird of special interest. It seems to prefer old-growth forests with a scattering of dead trees for nest building and feeding. Large and fairly rare, they excavate nesting cavities some 18 inches deep and up to 8 inches in diameter. The entrance is often somewhat rectangular to triangular in shape.

They prepare new nesting places each year so their old ones make ideal sites for other birds and some small tree climbing animals. The loud cadence of their pecking breaks the silence of the deep woods.

The common raven is a very interesting and intelligent bird. Somehow it always gives the impression of knowing everything that is going on. In the fall when hunters are about, the message gets around among the ravens when an elk is killed that food is available and just where. Their coarse croaking calls interspersed with chuckling sounds and now and then a few musical notes come about as close to bird conversation as we might ever hear.

The steller's and gray jays are not only very different in color but also in temperament. The dark blue steller's with its erect saucy crest and raucous voice are surely among the noisiest ones. They seem to enjoy imitating the whistling call of the red-tailed hawk. They also seem quite suspicious of man and his activities.

The lifestyle of the steller's jay is about as different as it could be from that of their mild mannered, quiet cousins, the gray jays. It is not unusual that camp is hardly set up before one or more of these unassuming little fellows drifts in. Their muted, whispering call is much in character with these friendly birds that appear to like people.

The sight of the dipper, or water ouzel, is always a special treat. The lives of these slate colored little birds are inseparably linked with the fast flowing waters of mountain rivers and streams. It is fun to watch them dive into rushing water and disappear to search for food along the bottom. They propel themselves through the water with their stubby muscular wings. Nests are made of bits of moss and grasses woven into a dome shaped structure. They are always close to the water, occasionally protected by the curtain of a waterfall. The dipper has been called as the only truly aquatic songbird.

I remember being pleasantly surprised one cold winter day near a rapid little stream well back in the wilderness. Snow was deep and ice coated the rocks. Here and there snow bridges had formed across the creek. I was carefully picking my way on snowshoes over one of these when I heard a sound that seemed to originate from the stream itself. When I looked more closely it was obvious it was coming from a bobbing little bird that was standing on one of the ice coated stones in the middle of the stream. I was being treated to the lilting winter song of the water ouzel. That moment I seemed to be hearing bits of a thrush's note and the plaintive call of a wren, all blended with the rushing sound of the stream. It is one of my most treasured memories of bird songs in the wilderness.

Another surprise was to find gray-crowned rosy finches high along the mountain tops, the homeland of the ptarmigan and the mountain goat.

Some of the other birds of the Bob Marshall that quickly come to mind are the thrushes, fly catchers, juncos, warblers, Clark's nutcrackers, kingfishers, sparrows, the flash of color that turns out to be the western tanager, the chickadees nuthatches as well as the diminutive kinglets. And surely we will not forget the hummingbirds.

Fishes

The Continental Divide separates the Bob Marshall Wilderness Country into several large headwater drainage areas. Each is quite distinct in regard to the fishes that are found there. All have had interesting histories.

The large Sun River drainage system flows through the wilderness on the east side of the Divide. There was a high waterfall on the Sun River at the lower end of the canyon outside the wilderness, but it is obliterated by the diversion dam. This falls may well have presented a historic barrier to the upriver movement of fishes. Early reports indicate there were few if any originally above that point.

Numerous early plantings were made. Brook, cutthroat and rainbow trout were introduced. Cutthroats seem to have preferred headwater streams. Brook trout have done best in the slower more meandering streams and beaver ponds as well as the West Fork of the Sun River. Rainbows are found most frequently in Gibson Lake and above, in the larger reaches of both the North and South Forks of the Sun River. Trout also have been planted in several small mountain lakes.

The Teton River system in the mountains is so cold and clear that it is not highly productive of fish foods. Although it is beautiful water, it supports a rather light population of rainbow and brook trout. There are cutthroats in the headwaters.

The fish on the western side of the Continental Divide in the Bob Marshall Country are predominantly native species. Much of the west side fishery seems to have been developed around an ancient rhythm of spawning runs from Flathead Lake up into distant headwaters. The two major fishes are the westslope cutthroat trout and the bull trout, often called the Dolly Varden. The mountain whitefish, although not involved in such long spawning runs as the others, are found in quite large numbers in the rivers of the area.

The original range of the westslope cutthroat trout has been drastically reduced through the years. As a result the Montana Department of Fish, Wildlife and Parks has designated this interesting and increasingly rare trout a Fish of Special Concern.

An important reason for its decline has been the alteration of its natural habitat outside the wilderness. The introduction of exotic fish into some of its more easily reached waters also has seriously affected the cutthroat. In addition to competition for food and space, the fact that the cutthroat readily hybridizes with rainbow trout has tended to eliminate pure populations, so important to the maintenance of its genetic integrity.

Because of its importance as a truly wild, native trout, coupled with its historical significance, the cutthroat has been designated as the Montana State Fish. This fine trout with bright red slash markings that have given it the cutthroat name, is sometimes spoken of locally as a "flat" or "blue back."

In the early spring, mature west slope cutthroats migrate out of Flathead Lake up the Flathead River and its tributaries. They may travel some 120 miles to spawn in the headwaters of the Middle Fork of the Flathead, well back in the wilderness. Since Hungry Horse Dam was constructed on the South Fork of the Flathead in the early 1950s, the spawning runs from Flathead Lake have been blocked.

In the Jewel Basin area, on the northwestern edge of the region, high mountain lakes are numerous. Cutthroat trout and a few rainbows are found in these small but beautiful bodies of water hidden away in lovely wooded surroundings.

Big Salmon is the largest lake in the upper South Fork being some four miles in length and half a mile in width. Cutthroat and bull trout are found in this body of water.

Several especially beautiful, glacier formed lakes lie along the west side of the Upper South Fork of the Flathead river drainage. For the most part, they contain cutthroat trout.

It is believed that cold, clear upper reaches of the South and Middle Forks of the Flathead River system in the Bob Marshall Wilderness Country form the last most secure stronghold of the westslope cutthroat trout. Its very survival may well depend upon these wild, unchanged rivers and streams.

The bull trout has shared these headwaters with the cutthroat and mountain whitefish for untold time. Until rather recently this big fish was locally known as the Dolly Varden. It has been found that the name Dolly Varden should be applied to its close relative, a large sea-going form living along the coast of Alaska and south to the state of Washington. Our bull trout spends its entire life in fresh water and is found from the state of Washington into Western Montana.

In the late spring, mature bull trout, sometimes up to three feet in length and 10 to 20 pounds in weight, leave Flathead Lake on their long journey to their fall spawning areas near the headwaters of the Flathead River system. An important share of these spawning waters is within the Bob Marshall Wilderness Country.

During their long up-river trek, these large trout feed upon mountain whitefish and any other aquatic creatures they can conveniently obtain. As fall approaches their coloration becomes increasingly bright. They spawn in September and October, often in rather small side streams. After spawning the mature bull trout have been found to return to Flathead Lake.

The fry emerge from the eggs in early spring. The young bull trout spend from two to four years in these tributary streams, which they share with young cutthroat trout.

Hungry Horse Reservoir is thought to be substituting to some extent for the previously available wintering waters of Flathead Lake for the bull trout of the upper South Fork of the Flathead River.

The beautiful wilderness region lying south of Scapegoat Mountain presents an interesting fish population. Rainbow, cutthroat and bull trout are found in the North Fork of the Blackfoot River and its tributaries. The Landers Fork of the Blackfoot with its side streams contain a wilderness fishery similar to that in the North Fork drainage. There are several beautiful mountain lakes in the area that contain cutthroat and rainbow trout. Arctic grayling are found in Heart Lake.

On the east side, the scenic upper Dearborn River supports predominantly rainbow trout with cutthroat in the headwaters.

It is truly a thrill to catch glimpses of large bull trout in deep, green pools of the Flathead and Blackfoot river systems. The flash of the cutthroat and the arching leap of the rainbow in the wild, unchanged waters of the Bob Marshall Wilderness Country surely add much to the vast variety of lovely living things up there along the nation's high divide.

Some Wildlife Memories
Who Bluffed Whom?

Many memories came back while I was preparing material on the wildlife of the Bob Marshall Wilderness country. Some of these anecdotes I would just as soon forget. Others evoke feelings I would like to savor again. I am not proud of how I reacted to my first close encounter with a bull elk. The best defense I have is that it was a long time ago. The affair took place in a thick stand of lodgepole pine well back in Bob Marshall Wilderness country. It was mid-September and the rutting season of the elk was in full swing. I had finished a day of elk range mapping and was heading for camp.

It was very quiet as I worked my way through thick little lodgepole pine trees on a game trail. All at once the silence was broken by the exciting, musical sound of a bugling bull elk. The trees were higher than my head so I couldn't see, but I guessed the bull was in a canyon below me. On impulse I tried to imitate the sound by whistling. It must have been a fairly good attempt as he immediately answered. My feeling of accomplishment turned to one of concern when his next bugle note sounded. It was a great deal nearer than before. I well recall the uncomfortable feeling of being made a target.

I didn't have time to ponder. The high-pitched, shrill sound that ended in several deep throaty grunts was much too close. I had been sizing up a dead snag nearby. It had no bark and looked very slick and the only branches were up near the top. I will never know how I got up that thing. My next recollection is of finding myself above the dense thicket that surrounded me. What I could see from there wasn't reassuring. The tips of his polished antlers were all I could see above the thick little trees, the bull was coming up the same game trial I had been following and was moving quite rapidly toward me. He stopped, although he couldn't see me any more than I could see him. I could hear his heavy breathing and he seemed to be listening to me.

It was very uncomfortable, hanging on to that old snag. After deciding things couldn't get much worse, I hollered. My voice didn't carry very well, but the reaction was immediate. The bull turned with a crash. I never did get to see more than his antlers, but judged he was a big fellow by the amount of racket he made bounding down the hillside through the thick trees and downfall.

I slid from my snag rather sheepishly, thankful no one had seen me.

The Snow Avalanche

During the years I was privileged to spend with animals in the wilderness, I saw several instances of unusual accidents. A couple linger in my memory.

It was January and snow was getting deep. I had spent the night at Indian Point on the West Fork of the Sun River. My plan was to snowshoe up Indian Creek to White River Pass on the Continental Divide.

After getting well up the drainage I noticed a number of fresh coyote tracks. They came from several directions and converged at a point I couldn't yet see in the canyon below me. As I moved to where I could look down, three coyotes dashed away. A couple of ravens flew overhead making their wild croaking sounds. What I saw startled me. There in the canyon bottom in a jumble of deep snow was evidence of a real tragedy. Elk antlers and legs stuck up through the snow. It appeared that about six bull elk had perished there. Coyotes guided by what they found above the snow had tunneled to feed upon what was buried beneath.

There was still evidence of how it had happened. Apparently a small group of bulls had attempted a late migration from the White River drainage on the west side of the Continental Divide across to the West Fork of the Sun River to winter. Bits of a trail still showed where they had wallowed through deep snow on the north face of Indian Creek. High above where I was standing their trail ended abruptly in the path of a snow avalanche.

I was there again, in early April, this time with my partner. We had come from the north, having spent several days snowshoeing along the base of the Chinese Wall. The snow was still deep up there. With the glittering ice and great snow cornices that had been formed out from the crest by winter winds, the Wall had been unforgettably beautiful.

We reached the head of Indian Creek about mid-afternoon. Coyote tracks again told us we were getting close to where the bull elk had died in the snow avalanche several months before. Ravens were still there, and something else had been added. They were big, sinister-looking grizzly tracks. As we stood quietly looking over the area, we began to make out a pattern in the tracks. There were many by the elk remains. The rest were on a padded trail that led through the melting snowbanks to a nearby outcropping of rocks. Up there the trail ended at what looked to be a den near the base of a small cliff.

Mingled with the big tracks were some very small ones. We could make out that two little cubs had played on the snowbanks during trips to and from the den. As far as we could tell no tracks had left the area. We began to feel a little uneasy. We were standing on an open slope, apparently just across a small canyon from a mother grizzly and her cubs. We hoped they were taking a nap up there. We didn't linger. On the way down the trail I suspect we were sharing pretty much the same thoughts.

Several bull elk had been killed in the snow slide. Coyotes and ravens had feasted during the remainder of the winter. Now with the first hint of spring a grizzly mother had emerged from her den. With her was new life, her cubs. She had found nearby a welcome banquet. Death and life were playing out a sad but hopeful drama in that remote place far up on the eastern edge of the Continental Divide.

An Elk in Trouble

On another cold mid-winter day, with snow getting deep, most of the elk had drifted to lower elevations where forage was more available. A few were still wintering there. They were pawing through the snow for grass and weeds, as well as feeding on willow and aspen tips. Some were even scraping off bits of aspen bark.

I was on Elk Hill on the North Fork of the Sun River looking down through a grove of trees at an object I couldn't make out very well through the rapidly falling snow. As I got nearer I could see it was a cow elk. Surprisingly her head had become firmly lodged in the v-shaped gap between two closely growing aspen trees. She had apparently been reaching up as far as she could to scrape off bark. She must have slipped or the snow gave away. In any event, as she fell her head had been wedged between two trees. She had been there for some time as the snow and frozen ground beneath her had been torn up in her efforts to pull free.

She was a perfect target for any passing coyote, and there were plenty in the area. Otherwise a slow death by starvation and freezing would have been inevitable.

I took off my snowshoes and climbed carefully up through the aspen to get above her. I got as high as I could and wedged myself between the two trees that were holding her. I pushed with all the strength I could muster and felt them give a little. It must have been enough to relieve the pressure on her head and upper neck as she jerked free. She stood there for a moment and then trotted away.

I strapped on my snowshoes and continued on down the drainage. I will never forget the warm feeling that went through me. By a rare coincidence that winter day I had been able to save the life of an elk, far back in the wilderness.

Recollections of a Dark Night

One of my first assignments with the Montana Fish and Game Department in the early 1940s was to carry out a field study on grizzly bears in the Bob Marshall Wilderness and so I am often asked if I have had any close calls with grizzlies. I had a partner, a big husky fellow by the name of Ray Gibler. He handled our little pack string as we moved through the mountains. He was great to be with as the going couldn't get too tough and he never complained about my camp cooking. One July we were camped in a little meadow up near the Continental Divide. It was a nice evening so we didn't put up our tent. As dusk settled in, we both noticed how nervous the horses were. The grass was good, but they didn't seem to settle down as they usually did. They kept lifting their heads and glancing back into the deep surrounding timber. Neither of us mentioned it, but I am sure we were both thinking there must be a bear. Some clouds drifted over soon after we turned in so it became extremely dark.

We were lying in our bed rolls about 20 feet apart. It must have been around midnight. I had understood that was the time grizzlies become very active. Our little campfire was completely dead. All at once I was awakened by a half muffled shout from Ray. There was little question in my mind that a grizzly had him. I can still recall my momentary reactions as I lay there in the dark.

Options flashed through my mind a mile a minute. Option one was to get down into my sleeping bag and lie perfectly still. Option two was to leap out and make a run for the trees. I had second thoughts about that as the trees were big old spruce with a lot of dead limbs and sharp needles, and I was sleeping in my BVD's. I like to feel option three would have been to try to figure out some way to help my partner, but I didn't get time to think about that. All at once the heavy breathing and thrashing about nearby stopped. Out of the pitch dark came Ray's booming voice, "Gosh darn, there is a mouse in my sleeping bag and it's bit heck out of me." Oh yes, I have toned down Ray's comments a little — otherwise it is a true story.

Elk. Ken Reynolds photo.

CHAPTER FIVE

Bob Marshall History

compiled by Rick Graetz

One of my goals in assembling this book on the Bob Marshall Country was to compile a kind of anecdotal chronology of this vast wilderness complex.

The Bob Marshall Country has always been wild country. Hence, it has passed through time in relative peace and has escaped the kind of events that make news or are otherwise recorded. The very nature of the people who traveled through this mountainous land also dictated that little of its history would be written. The earlier days witnessed the passing of Indians and mountain men. There were a few attempts at homesteading, notably in the Danaher Basin region and in Gates Park. And some prospectors no doubt searched in vain in the various gulches for minerals. In the late 1800s, horse parties — some private, others guided by outfitters — began visiting the country to take in its beauty, fishing and hunting. In many cases these people blazed their own trails but more often than not followed trails developed by game, the Indians and the first mountain men.

After the turn of the century, forest rangers of the newly created Forest Service began to patrol the back country. Very few of these people, and even fewer of those who preceded them, recorded much of what they experienced.

The Forest Service has made attempts to get some of these early-day rangers to record their memoirs on paper. Unfortunately, in the case of the Bob Marshall very few accounts have survived. The most notable have been those of Charlie Shaw and Clyde Fickes. Much of what follows, is reprinted from Forest Service Publications. The balance comes from conversations with people who knew of early-day events. It might be best then to label this section Historical Notes.

They will show the steps taken to create the Bob Marshall Wilderness, the origin of as many place names as I've been able to put together, the legislative acts, some notes on Indian trails and history, Forest Service cabins, fires, archaeological observations, and notes from former foresters. We'll also look at the man, for whom this country was named. Of course, no history of the Bob Marhsall would be complete without looking at some of the people who have worked to protect and expand upon this magnificent wilderness complex.

The Creation of the Bob Marshall Wilderness Country

by Rick Graetz

In 1897, President Grover Cleveland established the Lewis and Clark Forest Reserve under the provisions of the Forest Reserve act. The Forest Reserves were administered by the Department of the Interior. In 1905, the Forest Service was created along with the Department of Agriculture. In 1907, the Forest Reserves became known as National Forests. Glacier National Park was at one time part of the Lewis and Clark National Forest Reserve, until 1910, when the area was given national-park status.

On August 16, 1940, Secretary of Agriculture Henry A. Wallace designated the 950,000-acre Bob Marshall Wilderness. It was formed by combining three previously designated National Forest Primitive Areas, the South Fork, established in 1931; the Sun River, established in 1934; and Pentagon, established in 1933.

The boundaries of the original primitive areas seem to have been determined by hydrological divides. The South Fork of the Flathead, the Sun River and the Middle Fork of the Flathead are the three major drainages in the area. The Pentagon Primitive Area was often called the Big River Primitive Area, a name commonly given to the Middle Fork of the Flathead River.

The Great Falls Tribune, on February 24, 1934 reported plans to create the Sun River area. "Plan to Create primitive area on Upper Sun River approved by F.A. Silcox. Boundaries— Black Reef west of Allan Ranch, across North Fork Sun River—up Sheep Reef to divide between the Teton River and North Fork of Sun: thence northwest along Continental Divide to head of Basin Creek and west between West Fork River and South Fork Sun River: thence along Black Reef to North Fork Sun River." The Allan ranch referred to in this article is today the Klick ranch at the confluence of the North and South Forks of the Sun.

The following is a copy of the original Forest Service document recommending the designation of the Bob Marshall Wilderness Area.

```
U
CLASSIFICATION - R-1
Wilderness Areas
Bob Marshall Wilderness Area
```

BOB MARSHALL WILDERNESS AREA

A great "back country" mountain and mountain-valley territory lying astride the Continental Divide in the Flathead and Lewis and Clark National Forests in western Montana, as more definitely shown on attached map.

The area includes and is bounded coincidentally with the limits of "primitive areas" of several years standing established under Regulation L-20:

South Fork - designated May 20, 1931.
Pentagon - designated October 18, 1933,
              enlarged July 5, 1939.
Sun River - designated February 23, 1934.

These will continue to be called the South Fork Unit,
Pentagon Unit and Sun River Unit of the Bob Marshall
Wilderness Area, with minor changes of boundary to in-
sure that the titles are truly significant.

Establishment of a wilderness area composed of
these three primitive area units will involve no present
change in requirements, since the particular restrictions
added, at the time of their designation, to the restrictions under Regulation L-20, bring the provisions well
within the requirements of Regulation U-1. Advertise-
ment and 90 days' notice will not be necessary. The
condition imposed, as no. 7 in the designation of
February 23, 1934, for the Sun River Unit, making the
designation subject to the existing First Form Reclamation Withdrawal, will, of course, continue.

The aggregate acreage will approximate 950,000 -
area largely unsurveyed, the figure cannot be more
precise. Of this aggregate, approximately 8% in odd-
numbered sections in the extreme southwest part is
alienated.

There is no demand for timber. Range use by
domestic stock is limited to saddle and pack animals.
The tract is of highest importance for watershed protection, especially on the Atlantic side of the Divide.

The country has great and outstanding natural
and primitive allure, which has attracted constantly
increasing numbers of visitors even before its primitive area designation. Inspiring are the spectacular
scenery and undisturbed naturalness of the less rugged
main stream valleys. Despite substantial use in some
spots, wild life and good fishing continue abundant
everywhere.

The Sun River and South Fork Units are already
quite well known nationally as well as locally by all
interested in wilderness areas. Local public sentiment
has staunchly supported establishment of the primitive
areas, and no questions are expected in regard to the
change here recommended.

This area was one of the first in which "Bob"
Marshall made his explorations and hikes in this region.
He was largely instrumental in its continuance in
primitive condition. It is one of outstanding and well
known wilderness areas that was among the earliest
designated. It conforms fully to the ideal conception

of a wilderness area. A worthy monument, indeed, does
it make to his memory.

Appropriate favorable action is strongly recommended to redesignate the existing primitive areas into
one wilderness area as indicated.

August 10, 1940 _Fanni Kelley_
Date   Regional Forester

Approved:

August 15, 1940 _Earl H Clapp_
Date   Acting Chief, Forest Service

Approved:

August 16, 1940. _H a Wallace_
Date   Secretary of Agriculture

The Scapegoat Wilderness Area was designated by Congress in 1972 and the Great Bear
Wilderness was designated in 1978 along with additions to the Bob Marshall Wilderness. To
this core of the Bob Marshall Wilderness were added two important contiguous areas to
make what we call the Bob Marshall Wilderness Country. At the time of the writing of this
book, 1984, other additions to the Bob Marshall have been proposed: the west face of the
Swan Range, the Monture Creek region, and various areas along the Rocky Mountain Front
including Falls Creek-Silver King, Renshaw Mountain, Deep Creek, the Teton high peaks
and Choteau Mountain.

Bob Marshall
His Vision
Was His Legacy

by Sherry Devlin
reprinted with permission from *The Missoulian*

Bob Marshall is credited with singlehandedly adding 5.4 million acres to the nation's wilderness system, and in 1941, two years after his death, 950,000 acres of western Montana wilderness were set aside in his name.

The first snow that September was as unpredictable — and fierce — as ever.

In a few short hours, the season catapulted from late summer, across autumn and smack into the frigid middle of January.

Flowers and berries disappeared under the snowy blanket. Moss-topped boulders turned to icy blocks. The path muddied. Everything that made the forest warm and colorful had vanished.

Now, as nightfall approached, the young woodsman was soaked and chilled — and lost in a howling snowstorm high on the Lolo Trail, somewhere in Montana or Idaho.

"I stopped in the soggy twilight to look at the map," he later wrote, "and observed with concern a discrepancy between my imagined position and the compass. With a cold, shrinking feeling in my stomach, I went over in my mind all the instructions, every fork, in the trail, and could not recall a single dubious turn."

But young Bob Marshall had come West for a taste of the pioneer life, and a night alone in the howling winter wilderness promised just such an adventure. "On a snowy September night, a century and a quarter before," he remembered, "Lewis and Clark had been camped here, two years from the nearest settlement, winter closing in, food almost gone, meat unprocurable by the best hunters . . . And I was worrying about a single miserable night!"

Not only did Marshall survive his first scuffle with nature in the wintry Selway Bitterroot Wilderness, but he eventually weathered an Arctic shipwreck, a grizzly attack, scores of assaults on previously unclimbed peaks and innumerable grueling day hikes of 50 miles or more.

By his sudden death — of a heart attack at the age of 38 —Marshall was himself a legend, a 20th-century Lewis and Clark, the first white man to scale Alaska's central Brooks Range, a best-selling author, a radical bureaucrat and tireless advocate of wilderness preservation.

Marshall is credited with single-handedly adding 5.4 million acres to the nation's wilderness system and 16 natural reserves to Indian lands. He lobbied for preservation of Alaska's freezing winterlands long before other conservationists took up the cry. And in 1935, he was the catalyst around which the Wilderness Society was created.

In 1941, two years after Marshall's death, 950,000 acres of western Montana wilderness were set aside in his memory. Today, the Bob Marshall Wilderness is the acknowledged crown jewel of American wildlands — a fitting tribute to the man who once wrote: "We can afford to sacrifice any other value for the sake of retaining something of the primitive."

Born to a wealthy Manhattan family in 1901, Marshall spent his city-bound boyhood "dreaming of Lewis and Clark and their glorious exploration into the unbroken wilderness which embraced three-quarters of a continent."

"Occasionally, my reveries ended in terrible depression," he later recalled, "and I would imagine that I had been born a century too late for genuine excitement."

Then young Marshall discovered the reddish-brown reports of the "Topographical Survey of the Adirondack Wilderness," tucked away at the bottom of a bookcase in his family's summer retreat on Lower Sarana Lake, N.Y.

"Immediately, he became enthralled by the accounts of explorations in the mountains which surrounded us," wrote his brother George. "We determined to penetrate those mountains, which previously had been accepted as a scenic backdrop along the skyline across the lake."

At first, the brothers were content with walks around Lower Saranac. Then came the fish pond and pathless woods. Then the floating bog. "Every ridge and hollow and deer runway within the forest where we lived became familiar to Bob and he gave them such names as Found Knife Pass, Squashed Berry Valley and Hidden Heaven Rock," George remembered.

On August 15, 1916, the Marshall boys climbed their first Adirondack peak — Ampersand — a 3,365-foot mountain south of their summer home. Six years later, the Marshalls —together with old-time Adirondack guide Herb Clark — had climbed 42 of the region's 46 peaks above 4,000 feet. Eventually they climbed all 46.

Marshall had found his "genuine excitement."

Bob Marshall. Wilderness Society photo.

VOL. XXIII, NO. 24   WASHINGTON, D. C.   NOVEMBER 27, 1939

ROBERT MARSHALL, FORESTER — CRUSADER

No man ever rode the crest of the wave of life with higher purpose or more joyousness than Bob Marshall. In electing his way of life, Bob chose mainly those activities which would help to make life better for those who need a hand or would preserve the quality of naturalness of some of our wild land. His ability to walk sixty miles a day in any man's country, and to finish with a spring in his step, typified the zest with which he tackled everything. He was as interested in a whimsical "study" of the dinner-table conversation of lumberjacks as in the I. Q. tests he made on Eskimos and his studies of Arctic vegetation. He was as passionately devoted to the development of organization camps for outings for the underprivileged children as to the preservation of wildernesses where those of special vigor and love of solitude might find adventure. And never a thought of personal prestige in any of his projects or his gifts to good causes.

Death came with shocking suddenness. Bob left Washington Friday night, November 10, on the Pullman for New York for a week-end family gathering. He was apparently in good health, and was looking forward eagerly to the family reunion. His death was discovered on the arrival of the train in New York, and was evidently due to coronary thrombosis.

Men like Marshall can ill be spared. He was a force for many good movements. He had the mental and physical vigor to drive ahead and to inspire and arouse enthusiasm in others. His joyousness and his lively sense of humor were contagious. His capacity for friendship had no bounds. He was "Bob" to hosts — from Justices of the Supreme Court to his beloved friends of the Arctic. Surely no man ever had more friends to mourn him.

But Bob would not want to be mourned. His going was shockingly premature, but he was not afraid to go. He came close to death in Alaska last summer. If there is a Valhalla for the spirits of men, may Bob's spirit find there one of his beloved wilderness areas — something to bring forth that expression we often heard him use, "Gee, this is swell!".

F. A. SILCOX.

Chief.

"The sense of adventure which one gets in the wilderness reaches its perfection in the romance of mountaineering," he wrote more than 20 years later. "The glory of conquering a summit which has baffled humanity by its ruggedness throughout all the passage of world history up to the present moment affords elation to which nothing could equal."

Long before graduating from New York City's Ethical Culture High School, Marshall had decided on a career in forestry and conservation. "I didn't have the remotest idea what forestry was," he once said, "but I had vague notions of thrilling adventures with bad men, of lassoing infuriated grizzlies and of riding down unknown canyons in Alaska."

Then, too, there was the example set by his father. An internationally known constitutional lawyer and Jewish community leader, Louis Marshall led the fight in 1914 to retain New York's "forever wild" guarantee for Adirondack State Park. He was a pioneer in bird protection reform and spoke harshly against the country's "hasty dismantling of her natural heritage."

The lesson wasn't lost on his son. In 1920, after a year at Columbia University, Bob Marshall enrolled at New York State College of Forestry — where his father was a trustee.

But young Marshall still yearned for adventure. Immediately after graduation in 1924, he headed for a summer of mountain climbing and research at the Wind River Forest Experiment Station, near the Columbia River in southwestern Washington.

In the spring of 1925, Marshall received his master's degree in forestry from Harvard and again headed West — this time to the Northern Rocky Mountain Forest and Range Experiment Station in Missoula. There he stayed for three years working his way from junior forester to assistant silviculturist.

It was in Missoula that the Marshall legend began.

"A real greyhound" in the words of one Forest Service colleague, junior forester Marshall spent nearly all his free time in the backwoods of Montana and Idaho.

It was there, one September afternoon, that he wandered off course in a blinding snowstorm. And there, too, that he came upon a pair of grizzly cubs one sunny summer morning.

"I stood watching their unconcerned antics with great interest," Marshall wrote in his journal, "until all at once I heard a crashing noise behind. Wheeling around I saw a colossal grizzly, not 30 feet away, charging straight at me."

"'There's not to reason why, there's but to climb or die,' so I started on the run for a whitebark pine which seemed to offer the closest haven. Up I went, faster than my unaerial anatomy had ever progressed toward heaven. Up I went for about 10 feet, when in my haste I stepped too clumsily on a dead branch. It snapped and I flopped."

Marshall survived the grizzly sow's charge by playing dead. But he eventually contributed to his premature death by subjecting an already-frail heart to tortuous hikes in the Bitterroots, Flatheads, Missions, Cascades and Selkirks. Rarely was a day hike less than 40 miles; most totaled 50 or more.

"Up in northern Idaho, Bob decided to walk around the head of the East River drainage and back to the Priest River Forest Experiment Station," remembered retired forester Chuck Wellner in a recent interview. "When he got back to Priest River and discovered he had traveled only 45 miles, he walked another five miles down the road so he could log a full 50."

Ralph Space, retired supervisor of Idaho's Clearwater National Forest, told of a 50-miler that Marshall made from Moose Creek Ranger Station in the Nez Perce Forest to the Bitterroot Valley near Hamilton.

"My fellas told me that when Marshall came in over the divide, he was so exhausted he would stumble, fall, lay there for a while and then hike some more," Space said. "He kept a record of any time he hiked over 50 miles. He really drove himself to the extremes."

By the time he was 36 — two years before his death — Marshall had logged more than 200 wilderness hikes of 30 miles in a day, 51 hikes of more than 40 miles and several of up to 70 miles.

"Toting a 50-pound pack over an abominable trail, snowshoeing across a blizzardswept plateau or scaling some jagged pinnacle which juts far above timber," Marshall maintained, "all develop a body distinguished by a soundness, stamina and elan unknown amid normal surroundings."

And Marshall did indeed love the wilderness. "It is the perfect aesthetic experience," he told Nature magazine readers in 1937. "It is vast panoramas, full of height and depth and flowing color, on a scale so overwhelming as to wipe out the ordinary meaning of dimensions. It is the song of the hermit thrush at twilight. It is the unique odor of balsams and of freshly turned humus. It is the feel of spruce needles underfoot."

A personable man, "filled with humor," Marshall had little trouble finding wilderness converts among his friends. "He loved the feeling of wilderness — the animals, forests and waters," said ecologist-writer Siguard Olson in a telephone interview from his Ely, Minn., home.

"When Bob shared his feelings and experiences, whether in his writing or speaking, he had tremendous impact," Olson said. "If he had lived even a normal life span, the history of our country and its wild places would have been a different story."

But Marshall probably wasn't cut out to be a "true scientist," said retired forester Wellner, who now lives in Moscow, Idaho, after a long career as assistant director of the Intermountain Forest and Range Experiment Station in Ogden, Utah.

"His real love was the wilderness, not the office or research lab," Wellner said. "When I took over Bob's old records in Missoula, there were hundreds of notes scribbled on little scraps of paper. He just wasn't too keen on details."

Marshall also left behind hundreds of "tall but true" tales when he journeyed back East in 1928 to study for a doctorate at Johns Hopkins University.

"Like the one about the time we was going to a dance in Missoula," Willner said. "Harry Gisborne (the fire research pioneer) was a great friend of Bob's. Harry's wife, Alice, noticed that Bob had a hole in his sock right above the heel. So Bob got some black ink, painted his heel and went on to the dance!"

Seasoned by his years in the West, and by the first of four treks to far northern Alaska, Marshall wrote his most important wilderness thesis while at Johns Hopkins. Marshall called it "The Problem of the Wilderness." His admirers called it "The Magna Carta of the Wilderness Movement."

In the Scientific Monthly report, Marshall warned that the "shrunken remnants of an undefiled continent are being despoiled." Valleys that once knew "only footsteps of wild animals," now know the terrors of modern highways, he said. Gone is the ground cover of fresh sorrel and twinflower. Here to stay is "asphalt spotted with chewing gum, coal dust and gasoline.

"Within the next few years the fate of the wilderness must be decided," he said. "This is a problem to be settled by deliberate rationality and not by personal prejudice." What followed was a step-by-step rationale for the preservation of wild country.

Anticipating protests by timber companies, Marshall explained that "what small financial loss ultimately results from the establishment of wilderness areas must be accepted as a fair price to pay for their unassessable preciousness."

The doctrine of "the greatest good to the greatest number" does not apply to every acre on earth, Marshall said. "If it did," he wrote later, "we would be forced to change our metropolitan art galleries into metropolitan bowling alleys. The Library of Congress would become a national hot dog stand, and the new Supreme Court building would be converted into a gigantic garage where it could house a thousand people's autos instead of Nine Gentlemen of the Law."

What was needed, then, Marshall concluded, was "the organization of spirited people who will fight for the freedom of the wilderness." Without their help, "there will be countless souls born to live in strangulation," he said, "countless human beings who will be crushed under the artificial edifice raised by man."

The seeds of the wilderness movement thus planted and a doctorate in hand, Marshall fulfilled his lifelong dream early in 1931 — and left for a 13-month sojourn to the basin of the Koyukuk River in Alaska.

There he found Wiseman, a self-sustaining Arctic hunting and mining village of 77 whites, 44 Eskimos and six Indians spread over a land as large as Massachusetts and New Jersey combined.

Content as he never would be in Washington, D.C., Marshall mapped the Koyukuk drainage and much of the central Brooks Range. He scaled a long line of previously unclimbed peaks, named hundreds of geographic features (like Frigid Crags, Midnight Mountain and Blarney Creek) and relished in "the most glorious year of my life."

His return to the East in 1932 brought Marshall's greatest literary success, the publication of "Arctic Village." Forum magazine called it "the personal biography of a wilderness settlement." Others heralded it as a "valuable sociological document, fit to join the works of Margaret Mead."

But for Marshall, "Arctic Village" was a testimonial to all that is right about wilderness and life in the wilderness. "The inhabitants of Koyukuk," he wrote, "would rather eat beans with liberty, burn candles with independence and mush dogs with adventure than to have the luxury and the restrictions of the outside world. A person misses many things by living

Preceding page: Lake Lavale, Bob Cooney
*Opposite page, top: from the top of Pentagon Mountain looking south along the North Wall country. Dean Lake on the left. The North Wall is northeast of the Chinese Wall and not part of the same formation, Rick Graetz; **bottom:** the head of Red Shale Creek looking along the North Wall, Bob Cooney*
This page: Trilobite Lakes looking southwest toward Pentagon Mountain, Bob Cooney

Opposite page, top: near the start of the Middle Fork of the Flathead at Gooseberry Park. Trilobite Peak in the distance, Rick Graetz; **bottom:** *from the top of Pentagon Mountain, looking along the Trilobite Range; Clack Creek drainage is on the right and Dolly Varden Creek to the left, Rick Graetz*

This page, top: *Strawberry Creek and the headwaters country of the Middle Fork of the Flathead, Rick Graetz;* **bottom:** *Dolly Varden Creek upstream from Schafer Meadow, Rick Graetz*

Top: *the east face of Pentagon Mountain. Rick Graetz*
Bottom: *the Middle Fork of the Flathead River upstream from Schafer. Rick Graetz*

Top: beargrass below the Trilobite Range. Rick Graetz
Bottom: Todd Graetz enjoying wild huckleberries in the Great Bear Wilderness. Rick Graetz

Opposite page: Dean Lake and the southeast face of Pentagon Mountain. Rick Graetz
This page, top: from above the headwaters of the Middle Fork of Birch Creek, looking down on Big River Meadows. Rick Graetz
This page, bottom: the Big River Meadows. Rick Graetz

*This page, top: from above the Middle Fork of Birch Creek, looking west through Gateway Gorge. Pentagon Mountain is on the distant horizon, Rick Graetz; **bottom:** from the South Fork of Birch Creek looking toward Mt. Patrick Gass, Rick Graetz*
Opposite page, top: Barbara Bennetts skiing in the Cabin Creek country, Rick Graetz;
***bottom:** looking up Blind Creek from the North Fork of Birch Creek, Rick Graetz*

Opposite page: looking up the South Fork of Birch Creek toward Mt. Patrick Gass. Rick Graetz
This page, top: Scapegoat Mountain in winter, Rick Graetz; **bottom:** Gary Buchanan fishing the Dearborn River in the Scapegoat. Rick Graetz

Top: *Scapegoat Mountain from the southeast. Gus Wolfe*
Bottom: *from the top of Scapegoat Mountain looking northeast. Rick Graetz*
Opposite page: *beargrass and Scapegoat Mountain in the Scapegoat Wilderness. Rick Graetz*

Top: *the Scapegoat country near the head of Cooney Creek. Gus Wolfe*
Bottom: *Meadow Creek in the Scapegoat Wilderness. Rick Graetz*

in the isolation of Koyukuk, but he gains a life filled with an amount of freedom, tolerance, beauty and contentment few human beings are ever fortunate enough to achieve."

His return from Alaska also brought Marshall's first major report for the Forest Service -"The Forest for Recreation and a Program for Forest Recreation," part of the National Plan for American Forestry submitted to Congress in 1933.

Marshall was now more convinced than ever that America's wild lands were in jeopardy. "The universe of the wilderness, all over the United States, is vanishing with appalling rapidity," he wrote. "It is melting away like the last snowbank on some south-facing mountainside during a hot afternoon in June."

The solution, he said, was the protection of 45 million acres — 9 percent of the nation's commercial timberland. Of that amount, 3 million acres would be "superlative scenic areas" like Yellowstone or Yosemite and 9.5 million acres would be "primeval areas or tracts of virgin timber in which human activities have never upset the normal processes of nature."

A third category — wilderness areas — required set-asides of at least 10 million acres in Marshall's plan. "And by wilderness," he said, "I mean regions sufficiently spacious that a person may spend at least a week or two of travel in them without crossing his own tracks."

The remaining 12.5 million acres, then, would be divided between roadside scenic areas, campsites, forest residence areas and non-wilderness outing areas. And rather than ruin commercial timber interests, Marshall said, his plan would actually increase the value of their land.

The trick, he claimed, was proper forest management — which in Marshall's book meant nationalizaion of timberlands. "Public ownership is the only basis from which we can hope to protect the incalculable values of forest for wood resources, for soil and water conservation and for recreations," he wrote in "The People's Forests."

"The time has come," Marshall said, "when we must discard the unsocial view that our woods are the lumberman's and substitute the broader ideal that every acre of woodland in the country is rightly a part of the people's forests."

Retired Clearwater Forest Superviser Space spent many an hour debating the nationalization of timberland with Marshall. "We talked quite a bit about Bob's high regard for communistic forms of government," Space said. "He believed that goods should be produced for service, not profit."

And while socialist and communist theories were popular during the depths of the Great Depression, it was "unusual to hear a millionaire advocate that kind of system," Space said. Marshall, who inherited a fortune from his father, eventually left $750,000 to a foundation "for the promotion and advancement of an economic system in the United States based on the theory of production for use and not for profit."

(Marshall's will entrusted another $400,000 to his friends in the Wilderness Society with the stipulation that it would be used to "increase the knowledge of the citizens of the United States as to the importance and necessity of maintaining wilderness conditions in outdoor America for future generations.")

"He was a wealthy guy, all right," remembered Clyde Fickes, retired Northern Region Transportation Chief who now lives in Evaro. "He was a protege of Mrs. Franklin Delano Roosevelt and both of them had all kinds of money. If he wanted to fly to New Guinea, he didn't have to worry about it."

Still, Marshall preferred a simple life and in 1933 accepted the post of Forestry Director for the U.S. Office of Indian Affairs. There he pushed his wilderness work to the forefront, lobbying the Interior Department for more roadless areas, setting aside wilderness areas on Indian reservations and organizing the Wilderness Society.

He wasn't without his detractors, however. Once, confronted by a particularly reactionary congressman, Marshall fired off this response: "Because I've been out in the woods and up in the Arctic a good part of the past five years, it may be that the Bill of Rights was repealed without my hearing about it."

... [In] 1937 when Marshall was named Chief of the Forest Service Division of Recreation and Lands, he finally was in the right place at the right time to turn his wilderness advocacy into action.

Every roadless area of more than 100,000 acres should be protected as "primitive land," Marshall said. And for every proposed highway, irrigation project or lumbering job, there should be a comparison of values: "Do the increased benefits of this extension of civilization really compensate for the loss of wilderness values?"

Taking to the road with a fervor often unknown in bureaucratic circles, Marshall set out to "inspect" the wilderness he wanted to protect. In August 1937, the trek was to northern Minnesota for a weeklong canoe trip with ecologist-author Olson.

"Bob was full of enthusiasm for the canoe country," Olson said. "We paddled all through what is now the Boundary Waters Canoe Area and Canada's Quetico Provincial Park. He told me that something inside of him needed to get out in the wilderness — so that's what he did."

In 1938, the call went out to Mississippi where now retired forester Roswell Leavitt "left him off along the road so he could hike 10 miles or so through the second growth southern pines." Another week it was New Mexico and an impromptu hike through desert brush and scrub pine.

"It was a good way of life for Bob," his brother George later wrote. "He enjoyed people just as much as the wilderness and needed both. He had a splendid sense of humor, great gusto and infectious enthusiasm."

The summers of 1938 and 1939 also found Marshall back among the people of Koyukuk and central Brooks Range. On his final journey, Marshall was shipwrecked in icy Arctic waters. "What an awfully easy way to die," he wrote. "I kept saying to myself: 'Gosh, I wish I had time to think over all the swell experiences of my 37 years before dying — to have the fun of recalling them just once more before I go.'"

As fate would have it, Marshall had only a few months to live when he returned to Washington, D.C., after his final Alaska adventure. But in that time, he celebrated one of his greatest successes — adoption by the Forest Service of the "U" regulations, which prohibited logging in wilderness areas.

In November 1939, when Marshall died in his sleep while on a train to New York, his colleagues and friends were stunned. "If there is a Valhalla for the spirits of men, may Bob's spirit find there one of his beloved wilderness areas," wrote Forest Service Chief F.A. Silcox.

"He was the one guy who could always pull you out of the squirrel cage and make you feel again the excitement, importance and opportunity in what you were trying to do," added a New Republic editorial.

"With his passing the cause of wilderness preservation lost one of its greatest champions," said ecologist Olson. "He would not be surprised to see that the battle for wilderness preservation is still raging. But he would be disheartened to see that even an area named in his memory is under attack."

The Bob Marshall Wilderness, after years of relative quiet, has erupted recently into a major battleground between wilderness advocates and oil and gas companies. Industry wants the Bob Marshall opened to exploration and development; conservationists want it protected. The battle is currently mired in the courts and halls of Congress.

But Marshall knew the fight for wilderness would not be an easy one and, a year before his death, he penned what many believe to be his most fitting eulogy:

"We're all young enough that we'll probably meet many defeats in the next 50 years. It's even conceivable that when we die we still will not have won the fight. But win or lose, it will be grand fun fighting and knowing that whatever we do in the right direction will help eventual victory."

(Sherry Devlin is a free-lance writer living in Spokane. She previously worked as the Missoulian's natural resources and environment reporter.)

Notes on Indians Part I

compiled by Rick Graetz

The Kutenai, Kalispel, Pend d'Oreille, Flathead and the Blackfeet Indian tribes roamed the Flathead River drainage. Their movements through and around this country followed their migration patterns determined by their search for bison and salmon, cambium and bitterroot. Deer and elk also constituted one of their major food resources as they were plentiful in these mountain regions.

The Indians on the west side of the divide, and especially those in the Flathead Valley region, had to move eastward and through the present-day Bob Marshall in search of the bison. Some main trails existed as well as less-used paths. Many of these were utilized to avoid Blackfeet raiding parties that frequented the more heavily traveled routes.

In May of 1970, the Montana Statewide Archaeological Survey, Department of Anthropology, University of Montana, Missoula contracted with the U.S. Forest Service to do

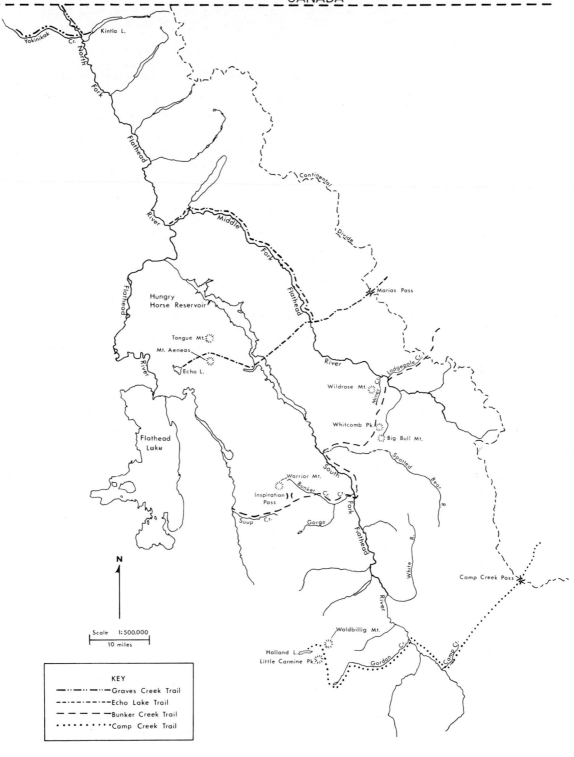

Early-day Indian routes as identified by an archaeological survey team. U.S. Forest Service photo.

About 100 feet from the Spotted Bear River, this ponderosa pine shows the scar of having bark stripped away to the cambium layer. Photo from Archaeology in Montana, Vol. 12, Nos. 2 & 3, 1971.

an archaeological survey in areas adjacent to two rivers in the Bob Marshall. Twenty sites were found: three of them on or near the Middle Fork of the Flathead, the rest on the South Fork of the Flathead River. Most sites showed evidence of short-term use while the Indians were passing through or hunting. Some of the sites identified are used today by horsepackers who frequent the area. Many of the areas show evidence of stripping trees to get at their cambium layer, a food source. Sacajawea told Lewis and Clark of this practice. Cambium was gathered in May and June; the favorite trees were the ponderosa, lodgepole, white pine and aspen. After the outer bark was taken off, the cambium was removed in strips, rolled and wrapped in leaves to prevent drying and stored for use.

Forest Service trails today have been planned to follow the shortest routes between two points with a minimum of elevation change. In most cases, trails follow river bottoms through timber and must be maintained. The Indians traveled differently. Their travel conformed to natural routes and they often followed the open ridge lines and high river terraces or game trails.

The archaeological survey crew identified two major routes across the Bob Marshall. They are easily visible, but today only animals use them except where they come in contact with current Forest Service trails. The northernmost trail began in the northern Swan Valley near Echo Lake and went through Jewel Basin to the valley of the South Fork of the Flathead crossing in a area now inundated by Hungry Horse Lake. From there it crossed the Flathead Range to the Middle Fork of the Flathead and headed northeast to Marias Pass.

South of Swan Lake, another trail went up Soup Creek in the area of Inspiration Pass and down Bunker Creek to the South Fork of the Flathead. From there it headed north to the confluence of the Spotted Bear River and the South Fork and then on up through the mountains of the southern end of the Flathead Range down Miner Creek to he Middle Fork of the Flathead and out through Lodgepole Creek over the Continental Divide into the valley of the Two Medicine River. The southernmost trail corresponds in many areas to the very popular trail from Holland Lake. This route climbed the Swan Crest from Holland Lake and then down Gordon Creek to the South Fork of the Flathead. It then headed south to the area of Camp Creek and the northeast over Camp Creek Pass down through Pearl Basin and the West Fork of the South Fork of the Sun River on its way to the prairie.

These trails have been documented. However, other routes are quite evident even today. If one follows the theory that the Indian trails followed the natural terrain then it is quite easy to find other routes across this wilderness complex. Many of the trails in existence today were either first used by Indians or the early-day trappers.

On almost every occasion that the archaeological survey crew left the river bottoms and moved into higher areas, evidence of early Indian use was commonplace. They concluded that perhaps this was further evidence that the Indians found that the easiest and quickest means of travel would have been on the high, open ridges. The researchers also believed that Indians used these areas because the game animals were there in the summer, it was cooler, and there were fewer bugs. Snowfields that existed well into the summer could have provided water in the absence of running creeks or streams.

As is the case today, many of the camping sites were found in the large meadows where horses could be grazed. Evidence from personal testimony shows that the Kutenai had a camp at Spotted Bear where they grew tobacco and hunted.

Much of the above information was provided courtesy of the U.S. Forest Service and from Archaeology in Montana, Volume 12, Numbers 2 and 3, published in 1971. I have intentionally not identified sites that might invite "pot hunting."

Notes on Indians Part II

compiled by Rick Graetz

Alice Creek was a major camping site on the historic road to the buffalo. Apparently Indians used trails outside the Bob Marshall such as ones through the valley of the Blackfoot, and then crossed over Lewis and Clark Pass, reached from Alice Creek. Lewis and Clark also camped in this area and crossed the pass on July 7th, 1806 as they were going east. F. W. Lander recorded crossing the pass in 1853. He was an engineer with the Stephens Rail Survey.

Another pass reported to have been used by the Indians in modern times is Lions Creek Pass, near Swan Peak and down Palisades Creek to the valley of the South Fork of the Flathead. This route was used by Indians coming across from the Flathead valley over Piper and Crow Passes in the Mission Mountains.

Another documented Indian trail went up the Spotted Bear River to the Pentagon Mountain area to Dean Lake, down Basin Creek, to Bowl Creek to the Middle Fork of the Flathead and then up Strawberry Creek to Gateway Gorge, through the Big River Meadows over Gateway Pass and down the South Fork of Birch Creek. Another trail used on occasion went over Smith Creek Pass in the Swan Range and down Little Salmon Creek to the South Fork of the Flathead Valley. Also recorded was a route up Trail Creek and Morrell Creek. This route was reached from the Jocko River Pass country of the Mission Mountains.

Pyramid Pass was particularly a popular route. In this case, the largest group of Indians camped in the Swan Valley and then sent smaller hunting parties over Pyramid Pass to Teepee Meadows and on to the Flathead River. Travois tracks are still evident in this area. The Teepee Park area is now called Leota Park. Hole in the Wall, also reached from Pyramid Pass, was another favorite campsite. A spot near here, on Kid Creek, was called Teeter-Totter Pass. The story goes that some Indian men were returning to camp and found the women and children playing on a roughly made teeter-totter. The Indians coming in over Pyramid Pass usually stayed for a couple of months from early September to late October. In the early 1930s, these hunting trips stopped. Some of the Indians died while in this region of the South Fork of the Flathead and were buried there.

Most of their camping activity was in the area now called Leota Park. From here they would hunt down toward the Big Prairie area or up into a region the Indians call Willow Creek. Today it is called the Danaher.

Big Salmon Lake, downstream from Big Prairie and just off the South Fork of the Flathead, was another favorite Indian camping area. The Indians caught fish here and smoked them.

There is very little evidence that the Indians stayed in the Bob Marshall Country year round. In the case of the Flathead drainage area, they tried to move out of the country by the third snow. An occasional tale tells of Indians not getting out before deep snow in the passes blocked their retreat, forcing them to stay in the river bottoms all winter. There is evidence in the Big Prairie Area that some Indians were caught by early winter snows. There is sign of heavy peeling of cambium for survival purposes.

On the east side of the divide the Blackfoot Indians used Camp Creek Pass coming up from the Sun River Country and the Augusta region to get to the South Fork of the Flathead.

Medicine Hot Springs at the confluence of the North and South Forks of the Sun River was a favorite Indian gathering place. The water in the area had medicinal properties. Later, white settlers began using these hot springs and put walls around the water. The water was about four feet deep and the temperature averaged about 86 degrees. Today this original area is caved in. The waters have been diverted to a pool for use of a guest ranch now owned by the Klick family. This ranch is a small in-holding in the Bob Marshall Wilderness border.

Indians also camped just downstream from Medicine Springs at Scattering Springs and in the Big George Gulch area along the Sun River. The Indians called the Sun the Medicine River and Lewis and Clark named it as such on their first maps. They also spent time camping near this region in the summers of 1805 and 1806.

There is very little evidence of Indians camping beyond this area of the Sun River for any period of time. Paul Hazel, who lived in the Sun River country for more than 50 years, speaks of finding arrowheads and artifacts in the Biggs Creek and Beartop area.

The Great North Trail was referred to by the Blackfeet Indians as the Travois Trail, and they followed it along the Rocky Mountain Front. Before their use, it was a route followed by migrating buffalo. Studies have shown that this trail perhaps extended well beyond the routes of the Indians and went as far north as Alaska and south into Mexico and perhaps farther.

In relation to the Rocky Mountain Front, the Great North Trail runs along the higher benches just below the Front. When the first cattlemen came to the Rocky Mountain Front region from the area of the Judith Basin on their way to the Sun and Teton Rivers, they found the trail easily recognizable by the travois tracks dug deeply in the sod. There are places where the travois marks are still plainly visible from a distance as grass filled depression or gullies running counter to the natural erosion pattern. In some places the trail is marked by stone monuments put in place by the Indians. Teepee rings still may be found at old camping spots along the way. Evidence of the trail may be seen near Green Timber Gulch, Wagner Basin and the Sun River Canyon, and again near Haystack Butte and the North Fork of the Dearborn River and Bean Lake. During the Blackfoot era, the trail had several routes. As it came out of the north in the Glacier Country, it split in the vicinity of the Sun River with one branch going down the Missouri River to where Fort Benton would be located and the other through Prickly Pear Canyon on its way to Helena.

Notes on Indians Part III

by Charlie Shaw

This was Indian country before the arrival of the white man. Blackfeet Indian country was to the east. Flathead Indian country extended from the valley to the west. These two tribes could never be considered very friendly or congenial toward each other and often met in pitched battles in this mountainous country. The Blackfeet had an abundance of buffalo to supply their wants, while there were no buffalo west of the Continental Divide, north of the state of Utah. The Flatheads crossed the mountains to secure their buffalo. The Blackfeet entered the mountains to their west to fish the mountain streams.

There are brief reports of major battles between these two tribes. David Thompson, one of the earliest white fur traders in the area (about 1811), mentions one battle that took place near the mouth of Morrison Creek on the Middle Fork of the Flathead River. In this skirmish the Flatheads, supposedly, lost heavily. A major battle took place in the 1840's in what is now the Bob Marshall Wilderness, in the vicinity of Camp Creek, above Big Prairie, on the South Fork of the Flathead River. The Flatheads had been to the prairie east of Augusta on a buffalo hunt and were returning with their meat and a few extra ponies. They were camped near Basin Creek. Scouts had been left behind to report on any activity or to ascertain if they were being followed by the Blackfeet. Soon one of the scouts charged into the encampment to announce that a large number of hostile Blackfeet were approaching the Divide from the east.

The Flathead broke camp immediately. Women and children moved the camp down the South Fork to the open meadows near the present site of the Big Prairie Ranger Station. The warriors and braves moved back up the creek, stationed themselves in strategic positions on either side of the canyon, and awaited their foe. When the Blackfeet arrived, on a signal from their chief, the Flatheads opened fire from ambush. Taken by complete surprise, the Blackfeet were almost annihilated. A few Blackfeet raced back over the Divide in panic. Ranger J.R. Hutchinson told me this story in 1934, while we were on a snowshoe trip on game studies in this area.

Camp Creek seems to have been a favorite camping site for the Flathead Indians. There were several prominent tepee rings on this flat. Many Indian artifacts have been found in this vicinity.

Large scars on many ponderosa pine trees are further evidence of the presence of early-day Indians. These scars are usually on the south or west side of the trunk of the tree, from 5 to 9 feet in height and encompassing nearly one-third of the trunk. The sapwood was never disturbed; only the bark was removed. None of the trees were ever girdled so as to cause them to die. There are many such scars on ponderosa pine in the South Fork valley below the mouth of White River, Murphy Flats, and at other locations. There are some on the Spotted Bear River trail between Flat and Bent Creek. There have been several reasons advanced for this work. Perhaps the most acceptable is the one in the Lewis and Clark Journals that mentions the Indians used this thick, inner bark (cambium layer) for food during periods when there was a scarcity of other foods.

There are Indian paintings at several locations just outside the Bob Marshall. Paintings at the junction of the North and South Forks of the Sun River appear to depict a symbol representing the Sun. Perhaps this is how the river got its name.

There is a cave at the base of Union Peak, just southwest of the present Schafer Station, that has the appearance of having been inhabited — smoky ceiling at the entrance. There is no record of this cave having been studied by archaeologists. The last time I was there (1944), the entrance was nearly closed by talus.

Indians used many different routes to the buffalo country on the prairies. One main route was retraced and posted in 1932 by Supervisor Kenneth Wolfe. This route is over Inspiration Pass from Goat Creek, from the Swan Valley, down Bunker Creek to Meadow Creek, down the South Fork, to the mouth of the Spotted Bear River, up the Spotted Bear and over Gunsight Pass, down Minor Creek, up Morrison, Lodgepole, over the Divide east of Big Lodge Mountain, down the Badger to the plains south of East Glacier. The route is still marked by a wooden sign near the mouth of Morrison Creek. There is also evidence today of the old Indian trail from the Flathead Valley over the Swan Divide; it crosses just south of Mount Aeneas, near Birch Lake.

The Danaher Ranger Station built in 1910. Photo taken in 1925. U.S. Forest Service photo.

A hand baler in Cayuse Meadows, Big Prairie Ranger District 1925. U.S. Forest Service photo.

Top: The floodwaters of 1964 going over the top of Gibson Dam. The 1964 flood was perhaps one of the most devastating in Montana's history. The dam held. Bureau of Reclamation photo.

Left: The building of Gibson Dam. Photo taken in 1928. U.S. Forest Service photo.

The Early Days, Part I

compiled by Rick Graetz

Charlie Russell, the well-known western artist, used to hunt frequently in the Sun River country and often camped in the Wrong Creek area. The current-day Klick guest ranch, known as the K-Bar-L, located near the confluence of the North and South Forks of the Sun River, was at one time called the Allan Ranch. Originally it was 40 acres of deeded land given to a civil war veteran. Ralph Allan initially was involved with Bruce Neal in establishing an early-day outfitting business. Later on Allan developed the property that is now owned by the Klicks. At the same time, Bruce Neal homesteaded near this area at Scattering Springs.

In about 1930, a CCC group was working near Hahn Creek to build a landing strip. The project was never completed, nor was the airstrip ever used.

The route between the North Fork cabin and the North Fork of the Blackfoot, the Kutenai Creek and the Scapegoat area was used for early-day sheep drives. Sheep also frequented and grazed in the Tobacco Valley, south of this region. The Tobacco Valley is near Scapegoat Mountain and the Drivefork Area. The Carmichael cabin, marked on many maps, originally was built by sheepherders.

Charlie "Kid" Young for whom Youngs Creek was named was an early-day surveyor and trapper who stayed in the wilderness country during the winter and came out in the spring by high water.

Near Big Prairie, there is a grave for a little girl with the last name of Roush. In about 1925, she became quite ill and her father snowshoed out to Missoula for medicine. Upon his return he found that his daughter had died.

In 1912, a phone line was constructed up along the North Fork of the Sun River to the gates park Ranger Station. Just south of here, at Two Shacks Flat, there were two cabins used by wood cutters.

In about 1910, a railway survey was conducted up along the Sun River. The route was projected to go up the North Fork of the Sun, over Sun River Pass, down Bowl Creek to the Middle Fork of the Flathead and out to Coram. Of course this never came about.

Chick Grimsley worked in the Middle Fork Country in the 1880s and often used wickiups for his camping. These are nothing more than crude lean-tos formed by poles leaned against trees for shelter. Some of these are still to be found.

The Upper South Fork of the Flathead River experienced heavy trapping up until the 1930s, but it then tapered off. Many old, crude trapper's cabins or their remains still exist.

The headwaters country of Badger Creek was one of the favorite hunting areas of Gifford Pinchot, a giant in Forest Service history. He was known to frequent the area in the early 1900s.

During the 1929 season a fire lookout on Desert Mountain in the northern part of the Bob Marshall country just south of Glacier Park, counted among his experiences seeing two square miles on one side of his mountain swept clean by flames in the short period needed for him to sprint 200 yards.

Reliable observers have reported somewhat peculiar conditions on high mountain tops just preceeding violent electric storms. A certain scientist recounts vividly an experience on Great Northern Mountain, in the Great Bear, when his party found rifles, geological picks and other metallic implements emitting sparks visible in full daylight. One of the picks is reportedly still there, left by the owner who quickly dropped it as the party ran for a nearby glacier to lie close to the ice until the approaching thunderstorm had passed.

Early Attempts at Settlement

compiled by Rick Graetz

The following information has been put together by reading various Forest Service publications and other historical documents, discussions with Allen and Mildred Chaffin and C. B. Rich, of Seeley Lake, Joe White of Choteau and Bob Cooney of Helena. Bob Cooney also supplied me with some tapes he had made of a discussion with Paul Hazel, a long time mountain-man of the North Fork Sun River country.

In 1899, H.B. Ayres, of the Division of Geography and Forestry of the Department of the Interior made a survey of what was then the Lewis and Clark Reserve. While traveling in the

North Fork of the Sun River, he mentioned that there was some grazing going on and a few cabins were visible. He also had the opportunity to travel in the Danaher Meadows area in the upper reaches of the South Fork of the Flathead. Tom Danaher and A.P. McCrea, most likely the first white men to settle on the South Fork, homesteaded 160 acres each in 1898. They built several structures, including houses and barns and put in hay and grazed cattle and horses. Climate, and poor yields of hay for their stock, as well as accessibility to the outside world caused McCrea to abandon his homestead and in 1907, Danaher sold his land to the Hunt Club of Missoula. The Hunt Club had planned to raise horses on the ranch but were effected by the same conditions as the two homesteaders. Sam O. Acuff eventually took over ownership. Later, the Forest Service took over ownership.

The Ralston brothers at one time, tried to develop a coal mine somewhere along the Middle Fork of the Flathead River. The attempt was unsuccessful.

There were other homesteads filed in what is now wilderness. In 1911, the Gates Park area was homesteaded and in 1913 several other tracts in the Danaher were filed upon but were not occupied. Climatic conditions and perhaps the fires of 1910, which burned much of the present wilderness area, probably influenced homestead entries.

In 1915, David H. Lewis, the District Ranger of the Big Prairie Ranger District compiled an agriculture report on the Upper South Fork of the Flathead. In essence his report said that the combination of severe winters, a short growing season, a limited number of farming acres, the high cost of developing access and the minimal chances of agriculture successes should dictate that this land is not suitable for agricultural activities. He recommended that all lands south of Black Bear Creek be closed to entry under the Forest Homestead Act. He also pointed out that the area's fish and wildlife values would be jeopardized by settlement. He felt that the area was of greater importance for attracting hunters and fisherman.

Lewis also pointed out that "the present routes of travel are trails, where it is only possible to use saddle and pack horses. The distance from Corum, a Flag Station on the Great Northern Railway, to Black Bear is 70 miles, to White River 83 miles and to Big Prairie 91 miles. The distance from Ovando, to the following localities is as follows: Danaher Creek 40 miles, Basin Creek 50 miles, Big Prairie 60 miles, White River 68 miles and Black Bear 81 miles. There are 15 miles of wagon road leading out from Ovando connecting with the trail to Danaher. The trails leading into this country from Corum and Ovando were constructed by the Forest Service and are very fair trails. They are the only routes of travel to the Upper South Fork."

The Early Days, Part II

by Charlie Shaw
from his book, *The Flathead Story*

Charlie S. Shaw, who at the time of this writing lives in Kalispell, Montana, put together a publication in the early 1960s for the Forest Service titled The Flathead Story. *Shaw worked for more than 31 years with the Forest Service beginning in the 1920s. Thirty of the years were spent in the areas of the South and Middle Forks of the Flathead River, now in the Bob Marshall Wilderness. This publication covered much of the Flathead National Forest. The excerpts that follow are about the Bob Marshall Country only. I have taken them exactly as Shaw presented them in his fine publication.*

In 1898 Forest Service Rangers roamed the mountainous terrain of the Flathead at a salary of $60 per month. They had to supply their own horses, bedrolls, and subsistence out of this pay. Examinations for Forest Rangers and examinations for Forest Supervisors were separate. It was possible, by passing the examination, to be appointed Supervisor without having worked for the Forest Service or having had technical training in forestry. At that time the wages for Forest guards was $60 per month; Rangers received $75 per month. Each supplied his own provisions, horses, camping equipment (including bedding), and horse feed. The following is an excerpt of a typical appointment letter: "Frank Opalka, May 23, 1906. You have been appointed to Forest Guard at $60 per month to take effect June 1. On June 1 you will report to Ranger Sullivan at the U.S. cabin near Coram with your outfit and supplies for 2 months. Tools and tents will be furnished by the Service. You will work under the direction of Ranger Sullivan on the South Fork of the Flathead. Unless otherwise ordered by this office, you will not leave the Reserve before July 31."

Col. Sievers, U.S. Army, made a trip through the South Fork of the Flathead River in the early 1870's, perhaps as early as 1874. The party was seeking a route for a railroad into this area. They killed an elk at Mud Lake for camp meat. This was the first report of elk in the Flathead country.

In 1903, The first constructed Forest Service trail extended from Ovando to the Danaher Basin, a distance of 21 miles.

In 1905, Flathead National Forest headquarters were moved from Ovando to one room in the Conrad Bank Building in Kalispell. Rent was $10 per month, including heat. Supervisor Page S. Bunker asked for a clerk to remain in the office during his absence. He preferred a man who could use a typewriter.

In 1906, the first Spotted Bear Ranger Station was built by John Sullivan.

In 1908, the Lewis and Clark National Forest was divided into two National Forests: Blackfeet and the Flathead. Forest Service crews constructed the first telephone line; the line went from Kalispell and Coram. In 1910, telephone line was completed to Spotted Bear. In 1912, telephone line was extended to Big Prairie. In 1914, the lookout was constructed on Spotted Bear Mountain. It was used as an observation tower until it was replaced in 1933.

In 1925, Forest Rangers A.E. Hutchinson, Roy Hutchinson, and Al Austin found the frozen body of a hermit trapper named Marshall in his cabin on Cabin Creek in the South Fork drainage. Marshall had ended his life with a pistol. He had been dead for more than a month when the Rangers discovered his body in February. They made a sled and hauled the frozen corpse 35 miles over the snow-covered mountains to Ovando.

In 1939, the first air drop of a Flathead National Forest fire camp was made in the Bunker Creek drainage.

In 1953, the 46-mile road along the west side of the Hungry Horse Reservoir was completed by the Bureau of Reclamation at a cost of $2 million dollars.

On June 1, 1898, Gust Moser at Ovando, Montana, received his appointment as Forest Supervisor of the northern division of the then Lewis and Clark Forest Reserve through J.B. Collins, Forest Superintendent, Missoula, Montana, Department of the Interior, General Land Office.

Early Rangers furnished the packstock required to move their provisions and supplies. But as the Forest Service grew, so did the job of packing. Soon the Forest Service had its own packstock, principally horses, and hired the men to pack them.

All saddles were "sawbucks"; the "diamond hitch" was used extensively. Usually two men with from 15 to 20 head of horses worked together on long trips, such as from Coram to Big Prairie which required about 2 weeks for a round trip. They didn't usually tail them together; they just herded them down the trail, one man on horseback up front and the other bringing up the rear. They camped in any spot with water and grass for the horses. Horses were turned loose in the hope the men could find them the next morning. These were long, hard days. The standard of living at some of these camps was not very high. It was not very pleasant when it rained or snowed. Packing continued this way until the 1920's, when the mules started to replace the horses and the Decker packsaddles replaced the sawbucks for general use in the Forest Service. The diamond hitch went out with the sawbucks. They were replaced by using "manta" on side packs, which was more convenient than top packs and the diamond hitch, and they are easier on the animal. The last diamond hitch that I can remember seeing "thrown" in the Forest Service was in 1928.

Mule trains also brought more standardized packing. Mules were tied together in a string: eight mules, a "bell mare," and the packer's saddle horse.

Early settlers took title to practically all the suitable land up on the North Fork of the Flathead and much of the land in the Swan Valley. Most of these areas remain in private ownership today. Except for the upper South Fork on Danaher Creek, the South Fork and the Middle Fork above the railroad were never filed on by these adventurous pioneers. Two homesteads of 160 acres each were filed in 1898 by Thomas Danaher and A.B. McCrea. These homesteads were purchased by the Federal Government after the area was included in the South Fork Primitive Area. Northern Pacific Railway land grants in the Upper South Fork were all acquired by land exchange and are now part of the Flathead National Forest.

Mickey Wagoner's homestead, above Martin City, was the farthest up the South Fork. There were no homesteads on the Middle Fork River above Bear Creek.

A special-use permit was granted on Morrison Creek, about a mile above the Three Forks cabin, in the early 1920's to a Denver attorney named Hunter. The Hunter family used it as a summer home until 1928. Today only the ruins of the cabin's rock chimney remain.

About 1919, a special-use permit was issued on Hahn Creek, a branch of Young's Creek, on the upper South Fork above Big Prairie, to Ruby Kirchbalm. After divorcing her rich physician-husband, Ruby fell in love with the "great out-of-doors." She bought a string of horses, hired "Smokey" Denow as a packer, and started a packing business. Ruby proved an able packer. Teamed with "Smokey", a rugged, Paul Bunyan type, Ruby Kirchbalm moved a lot of freight in the Flathead country. Often they packed for the Forest Service in the summer. They wintered their stock in the upper South Fork for several years. After 5 years, Ruby's interest in the back country paled. She returned to the East in 1924.

Just east of the Forest Service's Hahn Creek administrative site cabin, you can still see the cement "pad" where Ruby's cabin was built more than 45 years ago.

About 1919, Joe Murphy of Ovando started packing hunters into the South Fork. He always camped on the open flats below Holbrook Creek across the South Fork from White River. Today this area is known as Murphy Flats. The Forest Service issued Murphy a special-use permit for the area in 1922. He built some nice log cabins and a lodge. They served as his hunting headquarters until about 1937 when the permit was terminated by mutual agreement. The area was then in the South Fork Primitive Area. The Murphy's sons still use the area as their headquarters when in the area with fishing and hunting parties but the buildings are gone.

In the fall in 1949 when the Murphys were breaking camp near the end of the hunting season, their party consisted of 22 hunters, not counting Murphy's help. Each hunter had an elk. Murphy, his sons, and packers moved this party and meat, all in one trip. Each hunter had a saddle horse. Murphy's outfit is perhaps the largest and best that has used the Bob Marshall Wilderness for any length of time. Joe Murphy personally used this same area for 45 continuous years.

The Murphy and Kirckbalm special-use permits — first issued over 40 years ago — are the only ones ever issued on the South Fork above Spotted Bear. Creation of the South Fork Primitive Area in 1931, and subsequently the Bob Marshall Wilderness in 1941, precludes any permanent camps in this area.

Homesteading on the Great Plains and railroad construction brought a local demand for lumber and railroad ties. In about 1886, Charles Biggs and others built a wagon road from what is now Hannah Gulch up Sun River to Gates Park. This is now about 14 miles inside the Bob Marshall Wilderness. They proceeded to cut railroad ties on Headquarters Creek and Biggs Creek and float them down the North Fork of the Sun River. Their main camp was on Headquarters Creek, not far from Gates Park. They cut 200,000 ties and hauled out 25,000 cords of fuelwood between 1886 and 1899. The operation was not economical due to insufficient water at times in Sun River and the long distance to market.

Construction of Gibson Dam on the Sun River above Hannan Gulch in 1929 inundated several miles of the lower end of this road. The 14 miles of road in the wilderness have now grown over; the logging scars have healed and most of the stumps are no longer in evidence. It is again a true wilderness. However, following the logging operations near Gates Park, a homestead claim was filed in 1911. It was never occupied. In 1913, four tracts of land in the Danaher Basin were homesteaded beside the Danaher and McCrea homesteads of 1898. They were filed but never occupied. Climatic conditions, together with the long winters and distance to market over a rough trail, made farming and stockraising in these areas uneconomical.

In the late 1940's and early 1950's, extensive exploration by gas and oil interests brought pressure on the Forest Service for leases in the wilderness. The Forest Service objected to this exploitation as incompatible with wilderness preservation. The Bureau of Land Management, Department of Interior (the granting agency), agreed with the Forest Service. As a result, no leases were ever granted in the wilderness.

In November 1949, a severe windstorm blew down a large volume of timber in the Flathead National Forest. Englemann spruce, being quite shallowly rooted, was especially vulnerable to a storm of this intensity. Fallen timber provides an opportunity for insects to breed and incubate, especially the spruce beetle. An epidemic of these insects struck most of the major drainages containing spruce, including Bunker Creek, just north and outside of the proclaimed boundary of the Bob Marshall Wilderness.

While wildlife in the National Forest was always a concern of the early-day Rangers, wildlife studies were not started until the early 1920's.

Rangers traveled in pairs on snowshoe, usually with provisions and supplies on their backs. Cabins were few and far between; they made camp where night overtook them. These trips took from 2 to 3 weeks. Rangers counted the game in the areas they passed through and noted the condition of the wildlife and the condition of the winter range. They also checked for poaching or illegal trapping.

Dog teams were tried as means of transporting supplies on these game-study trips. These dogs and sleds, however, did not prove to be very satisfactory because much of the travel was on steep side slopes and through the brush off the trail. This system was soon abandoned.

The building of more cabins added to the convenience of these trips. Until 1928, the Three Forks cabin was the only building on the Middle Fork. This one and one-half-story log cabin

Top: Fairview Creek. Photo taken in 1925. U.S. Forest Service photo.

Bottom, in the North Fork of the Sun River country in the area of Two Shacks Flat in March of 1917. U.S. Forest Service photo.

Trail riders along the Chinese Wall in what was then the Sun River Primitive Area. Photo taken by K.D. Swan in 1935. U.S. Forest Service photo.

The Spotted Bear lookout in 1917. U.S. Forest Service photo.

was built in 1910 by Alen Calbick. Lumber for the cabin was "whip-sawed" near the site. It was used until it was damaged by heavy snow in 1956.

These annual game trip reports showed that the game had increased beyond the carrying capacity of the winter range. Some of the Rangers who carried on these studies were A.E. Hutchinson, Al Austin, M.B. Mendenhall, Fred J. Neitzling, Tom Wiles, J. Roy Hutchinson, Henry Thol, and F.S. June (Forest Service employee). There may have been others I do not recall.

In the early 1930's, it was realized that the elk population was getting too large for the winter range. As a result, a more intensive study was initiated in the fall if 1933. Three crews were organized to spend the winter in the area to study the problem. One crew was headquartered at Big Prairie, one at Spotted Bear, and the third on the Middle Fork at Schaefer.

The crews, with 6 months' supplies, went into these areas in early November and did not come out until late the following April. There were no plans for receiving fresh supplies or mail. Each crew carried a short-wave battery-powered radio for contacting the Supervisor's Office in Kalispell. Sometimes these radios worked. Crews heard from their families through the Forest Supervisor. I learned one day that I was the father of a baby daughter and that my wife and daughter were doing fine.

These men went through the usual dangers and hardships that go along with winter traveling on snowshoes in the mountains: snowslides, breaking through the ice in crossing rivers, short on rations, getting caught in storms, the cold weather (one time at Spotted Bear it was 57 degrees below zero), and camping out in the snow. These were all taken in stride. Perhaps the fact that there was a national financial depression had something to do with the men taking all of this in stride.

These wildlife studies were continued, in much the same manner, for the next four winters. The situation was analyzed and steps were taken to do something about the overstocked winter elk range. Spotted Bear Game Preserve was eliminated in 1936. The Montana Fish & Game Department extended the 30-day season to 75 days. Odds did not favor such large numbers of game; the winter range was greatly reduced; and, of course, the elk herd was reduced principally by malnutrition.

Following the four winters of intensive studies, yearly winter game patrol trips were made by the Forest Service through the area until 1941-42. Then, the Montana Fish & Game Department put crews in the area for winter study.

In January and February of 1941, Ranger Leif Anderson and I went through the South Fork from Coram and, after taking side trips up the major drainages, came out 32 days later at Ovando. We traveled on skis.

Some bears are quite smart. According to a story told by a crew at Schafer in 1938 (Schafer was then just a tent camp), they were having some difficulty in keeping their bacon away from the bears. In itself, this is not unusual. They put a long pole over a pivot in a fashion similar to a child's "teeter-totter." On one end of the pole, they attached a box for the bacon. On the other end, they attached a box of rocks, heavy enough to keep the bacon in the air. The box with the bacon in it had a rope attached; this enabled the crew to pull the bacon down when they wished. It worked good. They thought they had solved the problem, until a new bear came to camp. He would climb up the inclining pole and, as he passed over the balance point, the bacon box end came to the ground. The bear would then jump to the ground and immediately the heavier rock box dropped to the ground, raising the bacon up again. After several attempts of this kind, the bear left. Now, the men were more sure than ever that their contraption was a success. But the bear had not given up. He returned with another bear. The second bear stole the bacon out of the box as the other bear brought it to the ground. Of course, the bears got into a fight, but they had the bacon.

The Monture Ranger Station

reprinted from Forest Service files

The first Monture Ranger Station was near Shoup Lake on property belonging to the Anaconda Copper Mining Company and the Northern Pacific Railroad.

Before the Forest Service came into being in 1905 the area was administered by the General Land Office and called The Lewis and Clark Forest Reserve.

The headquarters for the southern half of the Lewis and Clark Forest Reserve was Ovando. There are few remaining records about the original Monture Station, but it is known that a Supervisor Bliss built a two-story house and a pasture fence on Section 31, about two miles south of the present Monture Ranger Station. The fact that it was not government-owned land apparently did not disturb Bliss.

Apparently, it did not disturb the Northern Pacific or the A.C.M. either. They had logged the area in the late 1890's and probably considered the land useless to them until time for the next timber harvest in about sixty years.

The purpose of the Monture station was to aid in fire control and it was not manned in the winter.

By 1911 the Forest Service was leasing the land for $10 per year from the owners. This arrangement was making Forest Supervisor David H. Kinney uneasy. Kinney counted $1,325 in improvements on the property and the land could be sold out from under them at any time.

Furthermore, since the Lewis and Clark Forest Reserve had split up into National Forests in 1905 and the Monture Station was now part of the Missoula National Forest, land had been set aside elsewhere for a ranger station. Certain parcels of land were set aside in each ranger district in 1908 for "administrative purposes" such as grazing land or fire lookouts or ranger stations. The land set aside for the Monture Ranger Station was in Section 20, about two miles to the north.

In 1914 John R. Toole of the A.C.M. informed Forest Supervisor Rutledge Parker that a private party was interested in leasing the land at more than when the Forest Service was paying. Parker, commenting on the situation, said, "It seems to me the government should own land in every case where the headquarters stations are situated. I am in favor of abandoning the present site and occupy(ing) the site which was originally set aside for a ranger station."

By 1920 a simple square cabin and some outbuildings had been built on the Section 20 land after the Forest Service cleared a space in the heavy timber.

The cabin built in 1920 served as ranger headquarters until 1927 when Seeley Lake Ranger Walt Robb and crew built the present station house and barn. Sometime between 1908 and 1927 the Ovando Ranger District was absorbed by the Seeley Lake District and the Monture outpost became part of the Seeley Lake Ranger District and is now a work center.

"Slippery Bill"

by Fred J. Neitzling
former Supervisor, Flathead N.F.

One of the most colorful Rangers appointed for seasonal work [at the turn of the century] was William H. Morrison, better known as "Slippery Bill." He provided his own headquarters at Summit, Montana, and was responsible for the Middle Fork of Flathead River drainage.

Grace Hansen wrote a "History of Flathead County — Great Northern Landmarks." In it she writes:

"Long before the railroad came to Montana a man named William H. Morrison held a squatter's right to a small piece of land at the Summit. When he heard that the Great Northern was extending its tracks through the Marias Pass, he installed a rosewood bar in his shack and was soon doing a flourishing business. The construction crews moved; but 'Slippery Bill,' as he was known, remained.

"Bill was about 84 when he died but before his death, he gave his small piece of land as a site for the obelisk in memory of Theodore Roosevelt. This monument, we hope, will be a landmark for many years to come, but we also hope that someone will keep alive the memory of the man who felt it an honor to give the government the land on which his shack was built, as a site for the memorial honoring the father of modern reforestation."

Bill acquired "squatter's right" to 160 acres of land at Summit. In the early '30s he donated this land to the Forest Service. Near the Roosevelt Memorial a large native boulder now carries a bronze plaque commemorating Mr. Morrison. He acquired the nickname "Slippery Bill" as a result of his astuteness in about 1890 during a poker game in a railroad construction camp at McCartyville — now a flag station called Fielding on the Great Northern Railway in the Middle Fork of Flathead River country. Bill won heavily and in the late hours of the game it appeared unwise to leave with so much money, knowing he might be followed by his gambling associates and robbed of his winnings on his way home. Pocketing most of his money and leaving a small sum at his place at the card table, he

Above, the Ford Creek camp in July of 1933. U.S. Forest Service photo.

Left, Three Forks sawmill taken in 1910. On top is Al Calbick, bottom left Dick Shields, and at the bottom right, Jack Clack. U.S. Forest Service photo.

a

b

(a) After the White River fire in 1919. U.S. Forest Service photo.

(b) Photo taken in the early 1900s. U.S. Forest Service photo.

(c) Trapper Bob Palmer with pack horses at "Medicine Cabins" on Arsenic Creek in 1908. U.S. Forest Service photo.

c

excused himself, saying he would return in a few minutes. Once outside the room, he hurried away and didn't return, thus earning the title "Slippery Bill."

Morrison Creek and Slippery Bill Mountain, a few miles south of Summit on the Flathead National Forest, are two features named after this early Forest Service pioneer.

Another incident attributed to Morrison is that quite late in his life, while at Summit, the trainmen would thoughtfully give him a daily newspaper and chat with him. He was a tall, stately old man with a long white beard and he became well-known as a rustic philosopher. On the depot platform passengers would promenade while the train made a 10-minute stop to take on water and undergo routine inspection. An eastern woman approached old Bill and inquired, "How do people make a living in this unpleasant, wind-swept, God-forsaken place?" Bill replied, "Lady, most of us make a comfortable living by minding our own business."

The Pre-Region One Days

by Elers Koch

Elers Koch, one of the U.S. Forest Service's innovative pioneers, was a native Montanan who took forestry degrees from Montana State College and Yale University. He entered government service in 1903, the beginning of a 40-year career that included 23 years as assistant district forester and chief of Division of Timber Management. Forest fire control techniques and formal training for firefighters were among Koch's many great contributions. He died in 1954.

When Gifford Pinchot in 1905 took over the Forest Reserves from the Land Offices, he took with them all the personnel, good, bad, and indifferent. The new Reserves, their proclamations fresh from the President's pen, had to be organized, and at the same time those already under organization inspected and checked up.

To that end, a lot of us young fellows in our twenties, with the vast experience of two years on the boundary job, were pitchforked by Pinchot into jobs as general inspectors and sent West to see what we could find out. Being a native son of Montana, my field of action was in Montana and Wyoming....

My first inspection of the old Lewis & Clark South in 1905 was an interesting job. This included the wilderness of the Blackfoot, Swan River, South Fork of the Flathead and the Sun River — and it was truly a wilderness at that time. Headquarters were at Ovando. The previous Supervisor had been Gus Moser, and many tales are told of his performances. It is alleged that he and his wife used to meet the rangers coming in for their monthly pay checks and mail, and that her wiles and other attractions, together with Gus' superior skill at poker, usually resulted in separating the rangers from most of their pay. Moser was succeeded by Bliss, who was Supervisor at the time of my inspection.

He was a nice old man, but quite incompetent, and his only excursions to the forest were drives in a buckboard over the only road on the Reserve to Holland Lake in the head of the Swan. Fortunately for him he had a ranger in Page Bunker. Bunker and I outfitted in Ovando with one pack horse and a saddle horse apiece. We rode up through the North Fork of the Blackfoot, across the range to the Dearborn, and north along the east side. Jack Clack (later in the Forest Service) was then buying Government timber and operating a small mill west of Augusta. We went up the Teton and down the North Fork of Sun River. We tried to cross into White River, but a snowstorm drove us out and we went back over the Dearborn. It was interesting that we saw no big game on that month's trip, though we ate grouse nearly every day, knocking their heads off with our 30-30 rifles.

As a result of my inspection, Bliss was removed and Bunker made Supervisor and headquarters moved to Kalispell.

In 1906, I made another inspection of the Lewis & Clark South. I started from Kalispell with one of the rangers up the South Fork. By that time the rangers had pushed a trail of sorts up river as far as Spotted Bear, and from the head of the river down to Black Bear. Between these two points there was no trail, but we made it through on elk trails as best we could. Again, in a month's travel in the late fall we saw no big game. Bunker was doing good work opening up the country with trails so far as his limited funds permitted.

On the 1906 trip I again crossed the main range and rode up the east side returning to Kalispell by a rugged trail along the Great Northern. I camped one night near Nyack, and during the night both my horses were run over and killed by a Great Northern train. I put in a claim but through neglect in following it up the case expired by statue of limitation and I never collected a cent from the railway company.

The Lewis & Clark North in 1905 included all of what is now Glacier Park and the country northwest of Kalispell. F. N. Haines was Supervisor. Mr. Haines told me how he came to be appointed. He had been active in Republican politics in his home town in Indiana, and one day one of the Senators from that state called him in and said, "Mr. Haines, I have two positions at my disposal. One is a postmastership, the other a Forest Supervisor in Montana. You can have either one." Haines said he did not know a spruce tree from a pine, but he wanted to go West so he chose the supervisorship.

First Plane in the Bob

from the Mountain Press book
Fly the Biggest Piece Back
by Steve Smith

The first airplane landed in the Bob Marshall Country in 1928, a few months before aviation itself was 25 years old. Pioneer Missoula flyer Bob Johnson was at the controls of the OX-5 Swallow biplane that landed on a narrow, short Forest Service runway at Big Prairie. His passenger, Harry Gerard, worked as private secretary to W. A. Clark, Jr., and was joining his boss at the latter's fishing camp on Bartlett Creek.

In his biography of Johnson, *Fly the Biggest Piece Back*, Steve Smith offers the exciting account of this first flight, as it appeared in a Butte paper on August 9, 1928:

PLANE THREADS WAY
INTO WILD SECTION
Ship Piloted by Bob Johnson of Missoula
Lands Harry Gerard at the Clark Camping Site

The heavily timbered country of the South Fork of the Flathead River, north of Missoula, one of the wildest spots in the Northwest, with its sea of treetops and frowning crags and cliffs, one of the roughest of mountain sections, has been invaded by airplane for the first time in history, with a landing being made on Big Prairie field, a forest ranger port completed in July.

Bob Johnson of Missoula, one of the intrepid flyers of the New York-to-Spokane air derby, aviation instructor at the Missoula airport, flew from the Garden City yesterday morning and in the course of an hour and ten minutes had located the camp of W. A. Clark, Jr., hidden far in the recesses of the forest, located the Big Prairie field, some 60 miles off the main road, and by dint of clever maneuvering among the pines and over them, landed his passenger, Harry Gerard of New York, guest of Mr. Clark at his Salmon Lake summer home.

Fire in the Bob

by Rick Graetz

Like any other mountain forested area, the Bob Marshall Country has seen its share of major fires. Large areas of burn scars are still very much in evidence today. Of particular note is the country along the southern half of the Chinese Wall, almost down to Moose Creek and all the way across to the White River. This fire occurred in 1910, the year of the greatest fires in history in the northern Rocky Mountains. In the year of 1910, fires were burning all over the Bob Marshall Wilderness. The White River fire jumped the Divide and burned down into the Sun River drainages as well as along the Chinese Wall. It has been estimated that this fire burned upwards of 75,000 to 100,000 acres. The same year, a much larger fire between 120,000 to 150,000 acres burned in the Schafer Meadows area.

Besides 1910, other major fire years in the Bob Marshall were 1889, 1903, 1919, 1926, 1929 and 1940. Since then however, acreage burned has subsided. The manning of lookouts, the development of the smoke jumper program, the use of fire retardants and better access to the back country have minimized these burns.

However, today there are some areas in the wilderness that are being labeled as prescribed burn areas. Naturally caused fires occurring under defined conditions will be allowed to burn. Fire, of course, is an important part of the natural ecology of the forest. Many areas have been cleared and are better wildlife habitat because of fires. In the case of the Chinese Wall and that of a major open area near Half Moon Park below Scapegoat Mountain the views have been opened up by fires.

Because of short growing seasons, thin soils, lack of seed and moisture, tree growth in some burned-over areas, especially in the high country, has been slow. Grass and low lying vegetation comes back rapidly. On the better sites, especially in the wetter areas, west of the Continental Divide and in the northern reaches of the wilderness, recovery is much faster.

At the divide between Rock and Moose Creeks below the Chinese Wall. Looking at the smoke cloud from the White River fire in 1919. U.S. Forest Service photo.

Photo, above, taken in 1957 of an area burned over in the West Fork of Jones Creek. This photo was taken before a planting project began, and shows that little reproduction had taken place in almost 40 years. U.S. Forest Service photo.

White River Falls (at left) on the North Fork of the White River taken in June of 1927. The burned trees are from the fire of 1910. U.S. Forest Service photo.

Forest Service Cabins

by Rick Graetz

In strategic and scattered locations throughout the wilderness, the U.S. Forest Service has constructed small cabins to support personnel patrolling the back country, for snow and animal survey work and for other administrative purposes. At Gates Park, Big Prairie, Spotted Bear and Benchmark, buildings are in place for use as work centers and, in the case of Spotted Bear, to serve as a ranger district. Until recently the Big Prairie site also was a ranger district.

There has been some question about the appropriateness of cabins in a wilderness setting. In some cases the pressure for removing these cabins has come from the Forest Service itself and from outfitters. Some critics argue valuable time and resources have gone into building these structures and that a long-range study should be made before destroying them. Others believe that time and money would be wasted by wilderness crews setting up camps if the cabins were destroyed. What happens to them remains to be seen.

The following is a list of a few of these cabins, including their cost and the date of construction.

Welcome Creek cabin was built in 1933 by George Purtilar and Hector Hoyt, seasonal Forest Service fire guards. The cost of the materials was $158.

Green Fork cabin was constructed in 1935 by Harry Taylor and Grover Morton, seasonal forest guards, at a cost of $568.

Pretty Prairie cabin was built in 1934 by Hector Hoyt and George Purtilar. The cost of materials was $694.

Indian Point cabin was built in 1934 by Mac McIntyre and other seasonal employees. Material costs were $568.

Cabin Creek cabin was built in 1934 by Paul Hazel and Harry Taylor, assisted by the summer fire guards. Cost of the materials was $793.

The first small **Benchmark** cabin was built by Ed Druckmiller, and the larger cabin was built in the mid-'20s. A wagon trail to carry materials went into the wagons had to be taken apart to get over Wood Hill in an area called The Steps.

The **Willow Creek** cabin was built in about 1924, and an older cabin before that, perhaps about 1908. The **Basin Creek** cabin was built in 1928, the **Danaher** cabin in 1932, the **Gooseberry Park** cabin in 1928, the **Pentagon** cabin in 1931 and the **Pendant** cabin was built in 1954.

In almost all cases the material was packed in by horse for each of these buildings.

Spruce Park Guard Station on the Middle Fork of the Flathead River, 1947. It is thought that a flood destroyed the station in 1964. U.S. Forest Service photo.

The Big Prairie Ranger Station taken in 1957. U.S. Forest Service photo.

Top, Spotted Bear Ranger Station July 1923. U.S. Forest Service photo.

Bottom, Three Forks Ranger Station in 1912. The Ranger Station was built in 1909. U.S. Forest Service photo.

The new Spotted Bear Ranger Station located at the mouth of Spotted Bear Creek. Photograph taken in 1926. U.S. Forest Service photo.

Forest Ranger, 1907

by Clyde P. Fickes
(Retired 1948)

Early in November of 1905, my cousin and I made a back-pack trip up the South Fork of the Flathead, looking for trap line prospects. We camped one night at Fish Lake and woke up in the morning to find about 18 inches of fresh snow and more coming down steadily. It looked like a good idea to take off for the lower country, which we did. At Beaver Park on the river we found a small tent standing and decided to occupy it for the night. Along about 9 p.m., having built up a good fire and lain down to try to sleep, we heard bells, yelling and horse noises. It turned out to be the Forest Ranger, Dan Sullivan, and his assistant, Frank Opalka, with a string of pack horses, bringing out the camps used during the summer. They were wet, cold and plenty tired and pleased to find a warm fire and some supper prospects. Also, Sullivan was suffering with an ulcerated tooth that was giving him plenty of grief. The next morning we helped to pack up and traveled with them down the trail to the railroad.

That was my first contact with forest rangers and their work, and the impressions received caused me to apply for work on the old Lewis & Clark National Forest in the spring of 1907. Appointed a Forest Guard on July 1 at $60 per month and supplying myself and two horses, I was assigned to a survey party on Swan River with D. C. Harrison of Washington, D.C. as Chief of party, and Forest rangers Jack Clack and Ernest Bond, as well as a cook. On July 23 and 24 I took the Forest Ranger examination at Kalispell and was directed to go to the Hannan Gulch Ranger Station on the North Fork of Sun River. It has always been my impression that I was not a very promising candidate for ranger to A. C. McCain, Acting Supervisor, while Supervisor Page S. Bunker was on detail to Washington, D.C. so he figured, "I'll give this kid an assignment that he won't want to accept, or else he will never get to Sun River and we will be well rid of him."

They gave me a badge, a USE BOOK and a GREEN BOOK and told me "When you get to Hannan you can take charge of the Sun River District." That's how I became a forest ranger in 1907.

I had discussed with Jack Clack the possible routes to follow. He had suggested the best route at that time of the year was to go up "Big River," the Middle Fork of the Flathead, follow the railroad until I reached the east side, and then south, across country, until I reached Sun River.

Leaving Kalispell on July 26, we swam the South Fork —which was high at the old Fitzpatrick homestead where the highway bridge is now located — and camped for the first night. Fitzpatrick heard my yell for help and came over in his boat. I unsaddled, put all my gear in the boat, lined my saddle horse behind the boat, intending to come back and get the packhorse the second trip — but he had different ideas. Jumping in, he almost beat us across the river. I camped with Fitzpatrick for the night and absorbed some handy information about what was ahead of me on the trail.

Most of the trail followed the old tote road, which had been used when the railroad was built back in the 90's, and in some places where the tote road had been replaced by the tracks, it was necessary to ride between the tracks for quite a distance, which was somewhat hazardous as one never knew when a train would want to use the tracks. That second night on the trail I camped about 3 or 4 miles east of Belton (West Glacier) on the old tote road grade near some old cabins where there was some good grass for the horses. As I was setting up camp, six men on mules rode through camp headed up the river. Told me they were a Geological Survey crew making a topographic map of the area. The next day I made it to Essex and camped for the night with Ranger Dick Bradley and family. The next morning Dick went with me to the ford across Big River; he doubted if the river was low enough for the horses to cross without having to swim, and the current was rather fast. Anyway, we made it all right without any difficulty and proceeded up Bear Creek. Camped at the Phil Gypher place at his invitation, as there was good horse feed, and we were tired. That night I learned a lesson I never forgot in afteryears. It was necessary to picket the horses so they would be available in the morning, and I staked them by the head. Sometime in the night I was awakened by a lot of moaning and groaning from the direction where the horses were. Rushing out to investigate, I found that the packhorse, in trying to scratch his head, had got the heel of a hindfoot shoe caught in the neck rope of the halter and was choking himself to death. I never did that again — even for a few minutes, and I always used a half hobble on one front foot. A year or so later, the Regional Forester came out with a circular letter saying that in the future, no claims for dead horses caused while staked by the head would be allowed. Seems like there had been quite an epidemic of such losses.

From Bear Creek we rode to the Lubec Ranger Station where Guard Dayton was stationed. Flies were real bad, giving the horses no rest, and I stayed over the next day to rest the horses. This was July 31, 1907.

The problem now was to get across the Blackfeet Indian Reservation without having to go in to Browning for a pass. Jack Clack had told me of a place near his ranch on Dupuyer Creek, where I could get through the fence and save 2 days' time, as it was a long day's ride to Browning. Camped at Wolf Plumes' place on the Little Badger that night. I had worked on the cow roundup on the Reservation the year before and knew these Indians. They were camped on Wolf Plumes' personal allotment putting up the hay. There were five or six tepees of them. A couple years before that, the Government had built for him a two-room log cabin and partly furnished it, and it had never been used — even one night. The old man took me over and showed me the cabin and told me to camp in it for the night. I thanked the Chief and he said to me, "You got pass?" I shook my head. He grinned, shook his head, and left me to make camp. There was a new six-hole Majestic stove in the cabin, and it had never had a fire in it. I didn't disturb its virginity!

The next morning I saddled up early and headed for the hole in the fence, which I found easily. The fence was five barbed wires on posts, one rod apart, and the so-called gate was at a place near the Rutherford ranch on Dupuyer Creek on a little rise in the ground. By letting the wires down on two posts the wires would be close to the ground so you threw your coat over the wires, led your horses through, and put the wires back up in place. This had been done so often that the staples could be removed with your fingers. As I rode away, an Indian policeman showed up and yelled at me, but I kept right on going.

I stopped at Jack Clack's home on Dupuyer Creek and then pulled into the little town of Dupuyer for the night. We were tired; it had been a long, hot day. A manger full of hay looked good to my horses. I went looking for a steak for myself. It was late — 10 or 11 o'clock — and the only light in sight was the town saloon and eating place. The bartender said he would raid the kitchen and see if he could find a steak or something. There were three men at a round table against the back wall, and I went over to "looksee." It was a poker game, and there was around $3,000 on the table. The county doctor by the name of Long and two ranchers were having at it. The bartender said they had been there since noon, and they were still there when I went in for breakfast the next morning. I saw the bartender a year later; he said they didn't quit until the doctor had all the money on the table. I knew the doctor quite well later on.

The two horses I had were small Indian ponies, and each one was carrying 175 to 200 pounds. They were getting leg weary; and as the previous day had been a long hot one, we didn't leave Dupuyer very early. Late the next afternoon we pulled into the Hoy ranch on Blackleaf Creek. Ranger Linc Hoy was not at home, but Mrs. Hoy invited me to make camp beside the creek not far from the house, as Linc might be home during the night. There was a Post Office called Raymond near the Hoy place. Hoy was a holdover Ranger from the Land Office days of the Forests. He was a political appointee from Philadelphia. The principal activity; consequently, he spent most of his time on the ranch. I got away from the Hoy ranch fairly early in the morning with some rather confusing directions as to the location of gates I would find on the way. Finally, I rode into the Godwin Ranch at the forks of Deep Creek and was made welcome for the night. The horses had a good roll and spent the night in knee-deep grass. Godwin was an Englishman and ex-sailor with one good hand, and the other, a steel hook on the end of his forearm. He was quite a talker and really gave me quite a lot of desirable information about the neighbors, the weather, and the doings of the Forest Rangers in that area. It was haying time, and he tried to interest me in helping him with his haying job. He was a little put out when I informed him that I would be the District Ranger at Hannan Gulch.

Left Godwin Ranch about 9:30 and finally arrived at the Hannan Gulch Ranger Station about 2:30 in the afternoon. It was quite a climb down into the Sun River Canyon on a narrow, winding trail, across bare slide areas made by deer and elk on slopes as steep as 60 degrees and more. Found the two one-room cabins occupied by Ranger McCain's family: his wife, two children, Mrs. McCain's mother, father, and brother. Assistant Ranger Henry Waldref was in charge of the Station when I arrived. Waldref was another oldtimer who was appointed each year for 6 months to patrol the forests and watch for fires. He had a mining claim near Lincoln, and his 6 months' wages from the Forest Service were his winter's grub stake. Henry was camped in a tent along the creek, and I joined him there. To him the job was just a summer's outing. He had been in the hills for years; and I sure picked up a lot of handy

Forest guard Clyde P. Fickes in August of 1907 at the Hannan Gulch Ranger Station. U.S. Forest Service photo.

Above, looking north up Hannan Gulch at the newly erected flag pole at the Hannan Gulch Ranger Station in 1908. U.S. Forest Service photo.

Below, Fickes' first camp in Hannan Gulch in August of 1907. U.S. Forest Service photo.

ideas about life in the hills and living off the back of a packhorse that have been useful to me all my life.

At that time, the Sun River Ranger District, with headquarters at the Hannan Gulch Ranger Station, included all of what is now called the Sun River drainage, then called the North Fork, the Deep Creek drainage to the north and the Willow and Ford Creek drainages to the south. At that time, the stream running through the town of Augusta was known as the South Fork of Sun River. What is now called the South Fork of Sun River was then known as the South Fork of the North Fork, and we also had the West Fork of the South Fork of the North Fork of Sun River.

The Ranger District to the south was known as the Dearborn Ranger District, with headquarters at the Elk Creek Ranger Station, where Eustace A. Woods was District Ranger. On occasion, he was known to his close friends as "Useless."

The Sun River country comprises some very interesting, not to say spectacular, topography. The river comes out of the mountains in a due east and west course some 8 or 9 miles and breaks through a series of five sawtooth-like reefs, ranging in elevation from 6,000 to 8,000 feet, with the river at 4,500 feet. The reefs are perpendicular on the east face and at a 45- to 60-degree angle on the west. Looks just like a row of sawteeth. At the junction of the North and South Forks, the river runs due north and south for some 45 or 50 miles and forms a beautiful valley with many open parks and side streams which head up against the Continental Divide on the west, part of which is known as the Chinese Wall, as spectacular a piece of country as you will see anywhere. Natives of the area are brown, black, and grizzly bear; blacktailed deer; elk; moose; mountain sheep and goat; and the usual run of mountain small fry. Cattle grazing was permitted on all the Sun River Ranger District except the West Fork of the South Fork and Pretty Prairie, which was reserved for winter elk feed. In May 1908, I counted and estimated that 500 to 600 elk wintered on the West Fork licks and vicinity. That was about all the elk in that area at that time.

The business of the district, which included all the forest from Deep Creek on the north to Ford Creek on the south, included 10 or 12 grazing permits for cattle on the upper North Fork, Beaver Creek, Woods Creek, Ford and Willow Creeks and along the boundary south of the North Fork. Also there were a few free use permits for wood on Willow Creek. A typical entry in my diary for August 13th reads: "Rode up Beaver Creek road to Willow Creek, crossed over to Ford Creek and then rode NE to Witmer's ranch. Range along Beaver Creek getting short. Posted 4 fire warnings on Beaver Creek. No fires. 8 to 5."

As a fledgling forest ranger on Sun River in the old Lewis & Clark National Forest, I had many interesting experiences. One of the most interesting was my first ranger meeting, held at the mouth of White River on the South Fork of the Flathead River from October 14 to 18 inclusive, in 1907.

On September 30th, notice was received from Supervisor Page S. Bunker at Kalispell that the meeting would be held. The supervisor had just returned from a six-months' detail to the Washington office and I guess he wanted to find out if his rangers could get around in the mountains satisfactorily. E.A. Woods, who was the ranger on the old Dearborn District, was in town at the same time I was and we agreed that, in company with Waldref and Guards Nixon and Converse, we would assemble at the mouth of the West Fork of the South Fork of the North Fork of Sun River and all trail over the Continental Divide together. Nixon had been over the route with a hunting party and was to be the guide. I call it a "route" advisedly, because there was no such thing as a located trail except along the main river. The appointed day of meeting was October 8th, but due to an unforeseen circumstance I could not get there. A.C. McCain had been appointed supervisor of the Custer and I had agreed to see that his outfit was shipped to him. Lincoln Hoy, the ranger from the old Teton District rode into Hannan on October 3rd with Mac's saddle and pack horses which had been at Lubec. Hoy prevailed upon me, when he learned of the ranger meeting, to wait for him while he went home and got his outfit for the trail.

We left Hannan the morning of the 9th and camped at the beaver dams on the West Fork. The others had not waited for us so is was a case of finding our own trail over the divide. My diary for the 10th reads, "moved up West Fork Trail, camped on top the divide under the cliffs. Jumped about 5 miles of logs. Bum trail." I was riding the best mountain horse I think it was ever my pleasure to fork. A gray mare, ¾ Arabian, 8 years old, that I bought from McCain, who had acquired her from Gus Moser (once a supervisor) of Ovando, via a poker game, so I heard. Sure-footed as a goat, never excited, could jump any log she could put her nose on and, best of all, was never known to leave her rider afoot.

The next day, October 11, we pulled down to the mouth of the White River to be the first arrivals at the meeting site. We beat the other party to the meeting place. They had stopped to try and get some elk meat but failed to do so; we ate bacon and trout. In camp on October

Preceding page, top: early morning along the West Fork of the South Fork of the Sun River looking toward Red Butte, Rick Graetz; **bottom:** *Bear Lake, Gus Wolfe*
Opposite page, top: *Looking down Youngs Creek, Rick Graetz;* **bottom:** *from the top of Prairie Reef looking toward the Chinese Wall, Rick Graetz*
This page: *The South Fork of the Sun River near Benchmark, Bill Lancaster*

This page, top: Salmon Lake, Rick Graetz; **bottom:** *the South Fork of the Flathead River from above Damnation Creek, Rick Graetz*
Opposite page, top: the Danaher Meadows, Gus Wolfe; **bottom:** *from the air, Big Salmon Lake in the center and the South Fork of the Flathead in the right corner. The Swan Range in the distance, Rick Graetz*

This page, top: looking down Hahn Creek, Rick Graetz; **bottom:** the Danaher from the air, Rick Graetz
Opposite page, top: from the top of Ayers Peak looking toward the Jumbo-Wood Tick complex, Gus Wolfe; **bottom:** on Basin Creek in the South Fork of the Flathead country, Gus Wolfe

This page, top: Hungry Horse Lake, Rick Graetz; **bottom:** *Barney Jette, Vitto Zdanys, and Fred Flanders atop the Swan Range and just below Holland Peak. Rick Graetz*
Opposite page, top: *Great Northern Mountain in the Great Bear Wilderness. Hungry Horse Lake in the distance, Rick Graetz;* **bottom:** *Stanton Lake and Great Northern Mountain, Rick Graetz*

Opposite page, top: from above the Swan Valley looking toward the west face of the Swan Range and the western boundary of the Bob Marshall country, Rick Graetz; *bottom:* the Pendant Lakes in the Swan Range, Rick Graetz
This page, top: the northeast face of Swan Peak and the Sunburst glacier, Rick Graetz; *bottom:* the Jewel Basin country, Jeff Strickler

Opposite page, top: *Rick and Todd Graetz hiking along the Chinese Wall, Rick Ridgeway;*
bottom: *big cedar trees in the Lion Creek drainage, Rick Graetz*
This page, top: *Holland Peak and the crest of the Swan Range looking south, Rick Graetz;*
bottom: *glacier on the east face of Holland Peak; Mission Mountains in the distance, Rick Graetz*

This page, top: *larch trees in fall on the west slope of the Swan Range, Rick Graetz;*
bottom: *east face of Swan Peak, Rick Graetz*
Opposite page: *Holland Lake on the west slopes of the Swan Range. Rick Graetz*

Top: *clouds in a unique weather pattern along the Rocky Mountain Front known as a chinook arch. Gus Wolfe*
Bottom: *the Cain and Buchanan families and Todd Graetz, hiking in the Dearborn Canyon. Rick Graetz*

12 were Rangers E.A. Woods, Henry Waldref, Linc Hoy, and Guards Converse, Fickes, and Chet Nixon. Saturday was spent setting up the camp. Each of us had a 7 x 9 tent; Sunday we went fishing. For the whole time we were camped at this place, old Henry kept the camp supplied with flat trout — 16 to 20 inchers. All we could eat and then some! Monday, October 14, Forest Supervisor Page S. Bunker rode into camp about 2:30 p.m. His first words before he got off his horse were, "Well, Linc, I didn't expect to see you here." Bunker rode a good-looking bay horse with an Army McClellan saddle with leather saddle pockets. It was legendary that Bunker never carried food or bedding; the Rangers were expected to supply what was needed. He was followed by Ranger John Clack, Spotted Bear Ranger District; Ranger John Sullivan, Coram District (Bull of the Woods); Ranger Dick Dean, Dupuyer District; Guard Hale; Ranger Ellis Hoke, Big River District; Guard Phil Clack; Ranger Dick Bradley, Essex District. Then on the 15th came Inspector D.C. Harrison, Washington, D.C.; Ranger Tom Spaulding, Missoula; Ranger Ernest Bond, Swan River District; and Ranger Higgins. There were several others whose names I failed to write down.

There was much talk led by Bunker and Harrison, and we ran a Ranger Station survey of a proposed White River Station. On Wednesday, the 16th we all moved down the river to Black Bear to survey the proposed Ranger Station and to look over a log cabin being built there by Jack and Phil Clack.

I was informed that Tom Spaulding would be going to Hannan with me. He was to do some surveys on the Sun River District and on the Teton and Dupuyer Districts. I was detailed to furnish transport for him as well as assist with the surveys. It was getting late, and storm clouds were showing up every day. On October 19 the meeting broke up. Snow was beginning to cover the high country so those from the east side — some nine of us —pulled out for home. No one wanted to buck the logs on the West Fork so we went up to the Danaher Ranch and crossed through Scapegoat Pass and some 16 or 18 inches of snow.

The White River meeting was where I first met Tom Spaulding, who was later to be Dean of the Montana Forestry School. Tom accompanied me to Hannan, as he had been sent from the District Inspector's office in Missoula to examine some June 11 claims and survey several administrative sites on Sun River and Dupuyer Creek. Tom was my first contact with anyone who even pretended that he knew something about forestry. He introduced me to Swappach and Pinchot's Primer of Forestry, books which I later acquired and read, or shall I say, devoured.

We arrived at Hannan on October 23rd, and during the next two weeks we surveyed administrative sites at Pretty Prairie and Palmers Flat, also June 11 claims at Big George Flat and Beaver Creek. Nixon, Converse and Waldref made up the survey party. Tom hired a team and light wagon from Nixon and we left Augusta on November 10th and drove to Dupuyer, camping at the Ranger Dick Dean ranch about 3 miles west of town on the 12th. Horses got away and I spent the next three days hunting them. On the 16th and 18th we surveyed a June 11 claim for a man named Riley. It was cold and windy and almost impossible to set up a compass or hold a chain without breaking it. On the 19th I put Tom on the train at Conrad and returned to Augusta and Hannan on the 22nd.

On November 6th I received a notice from the Civil Service Commission that I had passed the ranger examination and was eligible for appointment. On July 1 I had been appointed a forest guard at $720.00 per annum, promoted to $900.00 on August 1, appointed an assistant forest ranger November 11 at $900.00 and on January 1, 1908, promoted to deputy forest ranger at $1,000.00.

From the time I arrived at the Hannan Gulch Ranger Station, August 5, 1907, until September 22, my District headquarters was a 7 x 9 tent at the upper end of the hay meadow since the Ranger Station buildings, two 14 x 16 log cabins, were occupied by Ranger McCain's family.

The Hannan Ranger Station consisted of an old log cabin, 16 x 20, and dirt roof, a 14 x 16 hewn-log cabin with box corners, a log barn, corral, hay meadow and pasture — all taken from a former homesteader or squatter named Jim Hannan, who allegedly operated a station on the old Oregon-Montana horse rustling trail. The story is that Jim also liked beef steaks and occasionally butchered a steer, regardless of whose brand it might bear. Seems like the neighboring ranchers, led by one of the largest cow owners in the Sun River country, surrounded Jim in this old cabin and convinced him with a few "Winchester salutes:" that it would be advisable to do a little dickering if he wanted to continue life's journey. Bullet holes were still evident when I occupied the cabin. Old Jim agreed to leave the country and not come back. Shortly after that, maybe 2 or 3 years later, the Government preempted it for use of us Forest Rangers.

For a Ranger Station, no more isolated or lonesome spot could have been found. Visitors were practically unheard of for months at a time. The nearest neighbor was Johnny

Mortimer who homesteaded in the gulch named for him. Johnny was a recluse and a bachelor. He never went to town. He had complete surveillance of all approaches. It he was not in the mood and a visitor approached, he would simply fade away into the rocky cliffs behind the cabin and would not come out until the visitor left. Whenever I was going to Augusta, I would let him know. He would give me a list of anything he needed, and I always picked up any mail for him. Several old-time friends paid him periodic visits. Sometimes one of them would stay all night at the cabin, but Johnny would not come in.

July 1, 1908, brought about quite a considerable change in the organization of the U.S. Forest Service. Six Regions were established with the headquarters of Region 1 at Missoula, Montana. A considerable number of new National Forests were also created, one of the new National Forests being the Lewis and Clark National Forest, with headquarters at Choteau, Montana. It included the area east of the Continental Divide, extending from the south line of the Blackfeet Indian Reservation to, and including, all the drainage of the Dearborn River. Later on, the north end was extended through the Indian Reservation and the Great Northern Railroad became the north boundary.

On July 3, I rode into Augusta and learned for the first time about the change of organization. On July 7, I rode to Choteau, curious about what was going on and how it would affect me personally. Met E.A. Sherman, chief inspector from Missoula, who was in Choteau to set up the new Forest headquarters. Learned that Wm. H. Daugs, of Kalispell, would be the Forest Supervisor of the new Lewis and Clark National Forest. I believe that Sherman was the first Regional Forester of the new Region 1. Anyway, we had an informative, to me, visit and I returned to Hannan Gulch on the 8th. The Ranger District Post Office address was changed from Augusta to Elizabeth, which was located at the Jim Caldwell ranch at the head of Barrett Creek, a branch of Deep Creek. Mail from Choteau came direct to Elizabeth twice a week. Augusta remained as the supply point for Hannan.

At this time there was a mining claim on Lange Creek where there was some evidence of sulpher and related minerals, similar to those in the mineral warm spring at the forks of the North Fork and across the river from the Lange Creek claims. So I learned about mining claims reports made annually on all unpatented claims on the National Forests by examining Mountain Chief mining claim on July 9, 1908.

This was the year of extremely high water on Sun River, the highest on record to 1908. During the month of June and early July, my trips to Augusta and the Ford Creek area were, of necessity, made by way of the steel bridge northeast of Augusta.

About the most convenient facility connected with the Sun River District was the built-in bathtub with hot and cold running medicated water. There was a warm, almost hot, mineral spring at the forks of the North and South Fork. Over the years users of the spring had dug out a sizeable pool. There was a cave where the water came out. I took advantage of this convenience whenever possible. I was told by some of the old-timers that in the 90's, in the late summer and early fall, a hundred or more folks from as far down as Great Falls would be camped at the springs. It was a beautiful spot until the Reclamation outfit ruined it with Gibson dam. In the fall of 1907 I helped build a beautiful two-room log cabin on the flat just below the spring. When Gibson Dam was built, the cabin was moved up to Arsenic Creek and burned in the 1919 fire. Incidentally, there was a double log cabin on Arsenic creek known as the Choteau or Medicine Cabin, built by some Choteau men and used as a hunting camp in the fall. It was a convenient stopping place for all of us travelers. Then there was the Scattering Springs along the trail below Big George where I nearly always saw mountain sheep, especially in the winter. They seemed to love the watercress that grew there.

The next nearest neighbor was Bob Palmer who had a homestead just below the canyon of Sun River. Bob farmed a little, raised a few colts, and ran a trap line in the winter. I have some pictures of him taken on the high-water trail along the north side of the river. There was another trapper and handy man by the name of Sumner Franks who usually headquartered at the old mine cabins near Benchmark.

Now it was August and time to put up the winter hay for the horses. There was an old mowing machine at the station, source unknown, and I scrounged enough parts to put it in mowing order. I borrowed a harness, and my little old Indian cayuses from the Flathead did a fair job of moving the mower. By August 6, we had the hay stacked — 13 loads in all, 10 or 12 ton.

What about forest fires? Well, there just weren't any, that's all. I do not recall that we had any lightning to speak of all that summer, and it was plenty hot at times. Also, there were not very many people roaming around in the hills.

On August 11, 1908, I rode to Choteau to meet the new Supervisor, Wm. H. Daugs and learned that a two-room log cabin was to be built at Patrick Bottom just below the forks of the North Fork; and I was to organize the job. The Supervisor gave me the plans and list of materials needed. I returned to Hannan in the rain, which it did all day.

The only source of sawed lumber in the Sun River-Dearborn area was White's sawmill on Smith Creek, a branch of Ford Creek. So I rode to Augusta, then to the sawmill, and ordered the roof sheathing, flooring, and finished lumber needed for the cabin, most of which had to be milled. Also arranged to have the material hauled to the building site. This took 4 days, and it rained every day of the trip. In fact, according to my diary, most of August was wet and cold.

Early in September, the lumber and other materials for the new cabin were being delivered, and this was no small chore. The men, two breeds, who had a ranch on Ford Creek, had contracted to deliver the lumber to the building site. They really earned their money. They used the bare running gears of two wagons with two four-horse teams; and, at some places, they used all eight head on one wagon. The old road, over which they were attempting to haul the lumber, had been build back in the 90's when the North Fork was logged for ties and bridge timbers for the construction of the "Turkey Track" railroad from Great Falls to Shelby and Canada. There had not been any reason or funds for doing any maintenance on the road since then. Most everybody who went into that area used packhorses to transport any needed equipment or supplies.

Guard Cunniff and I set up a camp on Patrick Bottom, near a good spring and scouted Medicine or Arsenic Creek for house logs. We selected fire-killed lodgepole which was sound and straight, and we had no difficulty in cutting suitable house logs, 30 feet long with 10-inch tops. The problem was to get them down to the building site, a distance of about 2 miles. We found an old abandoned mowing machine with axle and wheels in useable condition, fitted a tongue to it, and we had a rig that would handle two logs at a load.

Now, you are wondering where did these abandoned mowing machines come from, and how did they happen to be so handy for our use. Well, back in the 90's, a man named Cates homesteaded on the North Fork at a place now called Cates Park; and it was possible to put up native hay most any place. During the railroad logging on the North Fork, the mowers were used to put up hay to feed the workhorses used on the logging job. That's how come. They just were not worth hauling back out to the prairie.

Oh yes, there is a story about the cabin location. When we, the construction crew and myself, first made camp at Patrick's, we all discussed where the cabin should be located from the standpoint of water, wood, drainage, wind and view. We had finally selected a clear grassy spot with good drainage, with wind protection from an aspen grove and located about 50 feet from a good flowing spring. The logs were decked alongside this spot. On September 22, Supervisor Daugs and a mining inspector named Booth rode into camp. The next day I guided Booth over to the Lange Creek mining claim, which he was to inspect. While I was away, Supervisor Daugs set a stake out in the middle of a windy flat and said, "Here's where we build the cabin" — without even looking at our selected spot! His site was 75 yards from the spring and without any windbreak, which is desirable in the Sun River Country where the wind blows at least half of the time. My guess was that Daugs just had to assert his authority. Anyway, we had to move the logs and other materials to the new site.

It occurs to me that our way of living and operating during the early days of the Forest Service would be of some interest to readers of this epistle who are accustomed to all the modern 20th Century means of living and operating.

When I left Kalispell, my equipment consisted of a regular stock saddle with a blanket and bridle and a saw buck packsaddle with a blanket and saddle pad, a pair of canvas alforjas (pack bags), a halter, and lead rope for the packhorse. Camp equipment, consisting of two long-handled fry pans, three tin plates, coffee pot, table knives, forks, and spoons, a hunting knife in scabbard, a .32 Special 1894 Winchester rifle with leather scabbard, my camp bed, and extra clothes, a yellow Fish brand slicker (raincoat to you) and a canvas pack cover 7 x 7.

My food supply consisted of a slab of Winchester bacon, 10 pounds flour, can baking powder, salt, sugar, canned tomatoes, corn, string beans and milk—three of each. This stuff made a packhorses load of about 180 pounds. It was packed in the alforjas which made two side packs for the pack horses, and the bed folded into a top pack with the canvas pack cover over it—rain and dust proof. Then I threw a diamond hitch (the one-man diamond which Jack Clack showed me) over the canvas cover, and we were ready to travel. The saddle horse carried the rifle in a leather scabbard which hung from the saddle horn, my slicker, and me, which weighed around 175 pounds, more or less. About one-half of our time was spent in travel with this kind of an outfit. Each individual used his own variation according to personal ideas and desires.

Cooking was done over an open fire, and you soon became accustomed to a regular routine of setting up camp. First, the horses were unsaddled and turned out to graze. Maybe you hobbled them or picketed one and turned the others loose to graze. Then you rustled some dry wood, selected a place downwind for your campfire, and got the fire started. Then you set up camp. Most of us carried a 7 x 9 tent with 18-inch side walls; this was pitched in a convenient dry place. The bedroll was spread over fir boughs, if you were inclined to luxury. By that time, the fire had burned down to a good bed of coals (only tenderfeet attempt to cook over a blazing fire). You ate, washed dishes, smoked a pipe or two or a cigarette, took a good look at the horses and probably, just before bedding down, decided for various reasons — poor feed, stormy weather prospects — to catch the horses and tie them up for the night. For various reasons, known only to a horse, they will take off during the night; and you have a long walk to find them. Sometimes you don't find them for 3 or 4 days; that's hard on the legs, not to mention your temper. In the morning you start a fire, check the horses, fix breakfast, pack up, bring in the horses, saddle up, and you are on your way.

In those early days you probably spent an hour or two cutting logs out of the trail or just clearing the way to get through to where you wanted to go. That was the way you lived in the field, as it is sometimes refered to. Old Henry Waldref had a homemade sheetiron folding stove that he packed with him. On a cold wet night, it would make a 7 x 9 tent almost luxurious living. Oh yes, most of us packed a sourdough can with us at all times. Couldn't live without it!

An Early Hunting Trip

from the diary of Jim Blair, 1915

Editor's note: The following are excerpts taken from the diary of Jim Blair, from Monida, Montana. In the fall of 1914 he hired Bruce Neal, then an outfitter and homesteader on the Sun River, to take him into the South Fork of the Flathead Primitive Area. The Gilman he speaks of was a station on the Great Northern Railway near Augusta. Bruce Neal was later to be employed by the State of Montana Fish and Game Department and has been credited as being one of the saviors of the Sun River Elk Herd. Neal was the first manager of the Sun River Game Range.

Jim Blair's original diaries were first given to Cecilia Klick. They are now in the possession of her son, Dick Klick. Dick owns the Klick K BAR L Ranch, a guest ranch situated adjacent to the Bob Marshall Wilderness near the confluence of the North and South Forks of the Sun River. It is in this area that Blair spent quite a bit of time.

A trip made to the South Fork of the Flathead River in 1915, with Henry Bannon, Art Bannon, Elizabeth Bannon, Henry's Daughter with Hems Blair, Ralph Allen, Bruce Neal, John Gordon and Joe Buck as camp help.

I shipped my horses and pack outfit from Monida to Gilman. I went with them. Also Joe Buck. We rode in an emigrant car. We went by auto and wagon from Gilman to Ralph Allans Ranch on the North Fork of the Sun River.

I shipped my pack horses and outfit by rail from Monida to Gilman. Arrived Gilman September 3. Went to Augusta, about 2 miles. Met Arthur Bannon of Portsmouth Ohio. I had one man with me, Charles Green. Stayed in Augusta September 4. We met our guide Bruce Neal in Augusta.

September 5 Started from Augusta, went about 18 miles, camped on Smith Creek. I went fishing. Caught 26 trout, Bannon and I went fishing another day. I caught 4 trout. Broke camp on Smith Creek and went to the Dearborn River. My horse fell on me, no damage. A Forest Ranger came to our camp and told us he would show us a shorter way to the Flathead River that would save us 2 or 3 days travel.

September 10 Broke camp on the Dearborn River with the Forest Ranger leading. He took us over a divide and down a creek and up over the divide which was very steep. The horses could hardly climb it. Camped nearly on top of another mountain.

September 11 Bruce's horse and the Rangers horse went back on the trail so did not get an early start. After going down a steep mountain the guides were not sure which way to go to get us down onto the South Fork of the Sun River. They put in an hour or so hunting a way to get down as was very steep. Finally we got down and then our troubles commenced. When we got to the River we found no trail. We worked our way down the River until about 2:00 when Bruce and I went ahead to cut trail. It was a hard country to cut trail in. Then it began to rain and snow and we got wet to the skin. We got about 2 miles cut and I went back to the horses while Bruce went on down the creek to find a trail that led over the mountain to the South Fork of the Flathead River. I got back to the horses about 4 o'clock so we went down as far as the trail was cut and made camp. Still snowing. We had to tie the horses to trees as there was no food. Bruce came in after dark and reported he had found a trail over the mountain about two miles down the River but very bad going.

September 12 Bruce and I started to cut trail. We worked hard until 12:00 to cut it through to the trail over the mountain. Then we went back and packed down to where there was a little feed for the horses. The horses had had no feed for 36 hours. Snowing every little while.

September 13 Bruce went to look at the trail over the Continental Divide. Every little while a flurry of snow. No sign of Ranger. Bruce came in late this evening and reported he had found a way over the mountain. Still snowing.

September 14 Broke camp about 9:30 and traveled in a blizzard all day when we got to the top of the Continental Divide we had to travel two miles on the very crest. Most of the time we could not see 100 yards. The wind was so strong we could hardly stand up. Every little while the horses would turn their tails to the wind, and we could hardly get them along. The trail was very steep, both coming up and going down. During the worst part of the trail Bruce's pack mare slipped and rolled down the mountain about 60 yards. The hash rope broke and let the pack off. When she got to her feet she smashed the pack saddle. We had to lash the pack saddle together and repack her on the steep mountain side in the blizzard and everything covered with snow. There was about 5" of snow on the Divide. We got down on the Flathead River about 4:00. No snow there.

September 15 Snowed all last night and nearly all day. Did not move.

September 16 The sun shone today and we dried things out.

September 17 Moved from Danaher Ranch down the South Fork of the Flathead River. The Flathead River is a nice clear stream with lots of trout in it.

September 18 Camped on the Flathead River. Rained nearly all day. Made camp in the rain. After supper Bannon and I caught 15 trout weighing from ½ to 1¾ pounds. Finest trout fishing I have ever seen.

September 19 Had a visit from a Mr. Farnsworth this evening. He is a guide and has hunted in this country several years. We are camped in what is called Big Prairie, although there is not much prairie as timber is scattered all through it.

September 21 Moved down the River about 10 miles; passed through a very pretty country. One piece of trail is dug in the side of a very steep mountain, about ¼ mile to the bottom. If a horse slipped he would go to the bottom and have a terrible tumble.

September 24 Art, Bruce and I went on an exploration trip today. We went to find Salmon Lake. Found it about 3:00. It is about 4 miles long and about one fourth mile wide. Very rough trail to get into it. Some say there are Bull Trout in it that weigh 30-40 pounds.

September 28 Art and I went fishing, Art caught 5. I caught 7 fine trout. We made arrangements to take a spike camp up on the mountain so we might get a goat the first of October when the season opens. We will have to pack everything on our backs.

September 29 Are camped tonight in a basin nearly on top of the mountain. It took us nearly 5 hours of hard climbing to get here. Each one of us had a pack on his back. None of us was used to backpacking and we got very tired. Green went back to keep camp on the river. We have a very nice camp. We took a bed-sheet and made a lean-to and built our fire in front of it. We cut bear grass for a bed. We had a time finding water for camp. Bruce went up to a little patch of snow and melted snow for camp.

October 2 Green and Bruce went down to the home camp today. Bruce came back about 4:00 for some more grub. It rained all day — Art and I stayed in camp. We heard some talking and caught a glimpse of some pack horses through the fog. When Bruce came back he met them. They were two Breeds who were packing in an elk they had killed near our camp.

October 3 Snowed nearly all last night. Still snowing this morning. About 4" snow on the ground.

October 4 Snowed all day steady.

October 5 Wrote some letters today and sent them across the river by Green who caught the party going to Deer Lodge. Green saw some fresh elk tracks. It has snowed lightly all day.

October 8 Looks stormy this morning — Art went hunting. We heard 3 shots from the direction he went. Bruce saw the Breeds. They said the Indians had killed their limit of elk.

October 11 Sunday — Bruce went up after the rest of the camp. I went up to the Indian's camp to get a pair of moccasins. Green got two pair and Bruce got one pair. We got the 4 pair for $5.00. Art and I looked up a new trail to Saln Lake. Snowed and rained.

October 12 Art, Bruce and I went to the upper end of Salmon Lake. Found the trail very rough. Sometimes would go ½ a mile to make a few rods. Did not get back to camp until 8:00. Rained nearly all day.

Above, the town of Augusta prior to 1900. Photo courtesy of Bob Cooney.

Top left: Wagon road along the Sun River in the late 1800s. Photo courtesy of Bob Cooney.

Bottom left: The Medicine Hot Springs near the Sun River. Photo take in the early 1900s. Courtesy of Bob Cooney.

October 13 Art and I went hunting for the last time. The boys dried out the outfit so we can start for Augusta tomorrow.

October 14 Broke camp this AM (10:25). We camped at the upper end of Big Prairie. Saw some Indians today. Lots of signs of hunters. Today has been perfect, about the only good day since October 1st. The Flathead River is clear as crystal and runs over a gravel bottom. Driving the pack horses does not muddy it.

October 15 Another beautiful day. Broke camp at 9:35. Made camp on Danaher Creek about 4:00. Made a long drive passed 5 or 6 hunting parties. Not a cloud in the sky. Saw a comet tonight.

October 16 Camped tonight on the North Fork of the Blackfoot River. Passed the Falls of the Little Blackfoot River. They are very pretty. Traveled nearly all day through green timber. Most of the Flathead country had been burned over. Timber was very thick but very little game sign. We are nearing the Continental Divide. Horse feed poor.

October 17 Broke camp at 8:15. Had a very rough trail. So steep in places a horse could hardly climb it. Traveled nearly all around Scapegoat Mountain. We climbed up until we were about 8000' and had to go almost straight down again. Traveled nearly 8 hours.

October 18 Traveled about 20 miles today. Reached Augusta. Had a wagon road nearly all the way.

Green got away with the horses October 21st for Monida. We had taken the horses down the Gilman on the 20th and worked until 11:30 pm taking the shoes off and carrying water to fill two barrels for the horses enroute to Monida. Had to carry the water about 200 yards. Green will go with the horses. I decided I would go to the North Fork of the Sun River with Bruce Neal for a while where Bruce has a homestead claim. We had 4 pack horses and 2 saddle horses. Just below the canyon of the North Fork of the Sun River the government is putting a big dam across the River.

October 25 A little after noon we got to *Ralph Allan's place.* Ralph is Bruce's partner. We stayed there until morning.

October 26 Went about two miles up the river today to Bruce's place. He has just filed a homestead claim. Nothing done on it as yet. Shorty the horse got peeved again today and scattered his pack. No damage. I took a hunt in the afternoon. Killed two Blue Grouse. Did not see any fresh sign of deer or sheep on the side of the river we are on. No elk allowed to be killed on this side of the river.

October 31 Ralph, Bruce and I went up the river to some warm springs. The Indians called them Medicine Springs. There is a cabin and bath house at the springs about 10x12. We had a fine bath. The water is just warm enough to bath in. One place there is a cave where the water is 2 or 3 feet deep, where one can take a sweat bath. The springs used to be quite a gathering place for the Indians.

November 5 Bruce, Ralph, Dick and I moved up the River to Patrick Basin. Saw a blacktail doe. We all fired about 20 shots but did not hit her. The wind blowing something fierce on the mountain.

November 11 Moved up North Fork about 18 miles. Rained all afternoon and nearly all night.

November 13 About 5" of snow this morning. Ralph and I went up the river to Ray creek, about 6 miles. Very heavy timber with lots of wind falls.

November 25 I hunted today. Saw a bunch of sheep with a very large Ram. They saw me a long way off, so I waited a while before following them. After I had followed about a mile I met Mud Townsend, Gold White and Everet White.

December 1 Ralph came down today with some hunters. They only killed one elk. I intended to pack in my deer but Bruce did not get the horses in time.

December 2 Oscar Hamilton took the hunters to Gilman in his automobile. I packed in my deer. Bruce packed in the other deer he killed. The Bucks were nearly the same size. Oscar brought out beer and whiskey. Everybody got drunk. Some of them did not go to bed at all. They kept on beating on frying pans for tom-toms. Sounded like a wardance of Indians.

December 3 I went to Great Falls with Oscar Hamilton and George Bickett in their auto. I guess it must have been 100 miles and we went some.

An Incredible Hike

The Paul Hazel Hike
by Bob Cooney
reprinted from *MONTANA MAGAZINE*

Editor's note: Bob Cooney wrote an article for MONTANA MAGAZINE in 1979 on Paul Hazel, often referred to as "Pinnacle Paul." He was well known by all who visited the North Fork Sun River country.

Bob told us that Paul hiked into the Sun River mountains from his home north of Choteau in 1920, and stayed for nearly 60 years.

During the summers he worked for the Forest Service constructing and maintaining trails, building field cabins, fighting fires and manning lookouts. His summer headquarters was the wilderness station at Gates Park on the North Fork of the Sun.

His winters were spent as a caretaker of a remote dude ranch at the head of Gibson Lake on the edge of the Bob Marshall Wilderness many miles from the nearest road; he lived by himself.

The following is an excerpt from Bob Cooney's article of an amazing trip Paul made through parts of the wilderness in the early 1930s.

I am sure every mountain range has its stories of extraordinary hikes and I often think of one up along the Continental Divide in early December quite a while ago.

L. J. Howard, a forest ranger, and I were on elk patrol in the Bob Marshall Wilderness. Paul Hazel, who had spent much of his life up there was helping us. He was an exceptional hiker.

We had spent the night at a little cabin on Cabin Creek on the North Fork of the Sun River. Our plan was to cover the winter elk range on the North Fork up to Gates Park that day. Snow was still fairly light along the river, so we weren't using snowshoes. Each of us planned to cover a different area and meet that evening at Gates Park.

We had no idea what sort of ordeal lay ahead for Paul as we parted that morning. He was to cross the river and go up Moose Creek several miles, check on any game, take snow-depth readings and head north through the timber to the Gates Park cabin.

L. J. and I got in to camp around dusk. There was no Paul. We waited to eat supper and still no Paul. He was a superb woodsman and knew the area intimately. We couldn't imagine what might have happened. Much as we wanted to get out there we believed it would be best to wait till daylight to start a search for him.

It was well after midnight when the Forest phone jingled. The only line working at that time was one to the Spotted Bear Ranger Station way over on the South Fork of the Flathead River. It was Paul. He said he was calling from the old iron field phone up on the Continental Divide on Spotted Bear Pass.

He had found an unexpectedly large band of elk up Moose Creek. Tracks indicated they might have recently migrated across the Divide from the White River area. Paul thought it was essential to our work to verify this. So he headed on up Moose Creek. It was many miles to the Chinese Wall and snow got deeper the higher he went. He found the snow so deep along the base of the Wall that he believed it would be better to get up on top to head north to the pass he wanted to check. He managed to work his way up through the steep little pass at the head of Moose Creek. It was getting dark up there on top. He found the wind had blown the crest fairly free of snow. There was no trail and he had no light, but he made his way several miles along the top of the Continental Divide to an elk migration trail just south of Larch Hill. To think about how he got down off that end of the Wall through the snow cornices makes me shudder. In the dim light of the stars he could make out by tracks that a large group of elk recently had crossed the pass from the west side of the Continental Divide. This was the information he had worked so hard to verify.

He then made his way through deep snow around the shoulder of Larch Hill and on to the field phone at Spotted Bear Pass. There were still many miles to go to our camp down Rock Creek through heavy timber and snow. On the phone we had suggested he find a sheltered place, build a fire and wait till daylight. We said we would head up that way to give him a hand by breaking trail.

We were just about to leave when we saw Paul come out of the timber across the meadow. The Gates Park cabin, in the first gray light of the morning with smoke drifting out of the chimney must have looked good to Paul. I know he looked mighty good to us.

L. J. and I tried to figure how far he had hiked that day and night. He had traveled up Moose Creek much of the way in the snow without snowshoes. He had searched his way in the dark with no light along the crest of the Chinese Wall on the Continental Divide. There was no trail and a thousand-foot drop off to the east. Then there were all those miles down Rock Creek. He had hiked through deep timber where it was so dark that here and there he had to feel for blazes on the trees to make sure he was still on the snow covered trail.

He must have hiked nearly 40 miles.

Paul has always been a man of few words. His only reference to the difficulty of the trip was his comment after breakfast:

"I guess maybe I'll stay in today and wash some clothes."

Shoulders to the Wheel

The People of the Bob Marshall Country
by Jim Posewitz

The spirits of many people dwell in this wild land. They haunt the deep shadows of the spruce thickets. Their souls sing across barren ridges and murmur among the pines. Their ashes mingle silently in the duff of the forest floor. There are the memories and mortal substance of people who gave of themselves and sustained the life of one of America's noblest concepts — the preservation of wilderness.

Men are bonded to the earth. The American farmer turning furrow after endless furrow loves his "place," enduring anything to keep it. Cowmen appreciate grass, and swell with pride over the spread of their prairie. Wild land, too, is loved — passionately. It is a love that drives conservationists from every stratum of American society to gather or go singly on crusades of preservation. It has been so in the Bob Marshall Country for generations. Always there have been people who cared enough to stand and defend this place. Each challenge was answered, each gauntlet thrown was picked up, each thrust parried.

Archaeologists tell us modern man has roamed this planet since about 35,000 B.C. Within the last century, the human concept of preserving a small part of what we were given emerged. This idea grew to reality in perhaps the only nation where free men had a fighting chance to make it happen. In making preservation happen, it was seldom, if ever, a matter of men joining a popular cause. Rather, it seemed to be someone fighting for an ideal that challenged the momentum of exploitative forces of awesome dimension. In a pioneering nation, wilderness was to be conquered. At first, only a few chose to challenge that conventional wisdom.

Today, the beginnings of the preservation movement — the effort to stop the total conquest — are still in sight. The tracks laid down by the founding fathers are still etched plainly in the sand. The blaze marks left in their pioneering are visible. Saplings that bent at their passing now stand rigidly in today's gale. The trail is visible.

Many people have trod these tortuous courses. It is not the purpose of this chapter to print the roster of all who answered when the land lay vulnerable and threatened. The purpose is only to touch on a few who seized opportunity and history and at some moment declared, this land shall not perish, shall not fade, this land shall remain as God created it and as free men will it to remain.

In time, many chronicles will add to the history and the truth of the preservation of the Bob Marshall Country. The list of heroes in the struggle will grow; time will eventually call up all the right names. This chapter will retell the tale of a few who forged solid links in the chain of events that preserved this masterpiece of genesis. They are offered as testimony; for each person who cares there will be a time and place to forge a new link and answer yet another challenge. Should the recorders of events fail and leave some deed without proper notice, there is the greater comfort in knowing the land will not forget. This land will forever stand in remembrance of each and every contribution; its future, a total reflection of every person's deed.

Three major battles and a hundred skirmishes have molded the Bob Marshall Country. The centerpiece was born in the minds of men who loved just plain wilderness and simultaneously, in the hearts of people striving to protect and restore the wildlife of the Northern Rockies.

Any discussion of the people who held the land for us must start with the man himself, Bob Marshall. A Forest Service (FS) professional, he was a tireless and successful advocate for wild land within his agency. It was a time when such advocacy was tolerated and could be successful. The agency viewed itself as protector of the forest first and accommodator of exploitative uses second. It was an attitude that would change before the Lincoln-Scapegoat was added to the Bob Marshall Country.

In the late 1920s, Bob Marshall was assistant silviculturist at the Forest Service's Northern Rocky Mountain Forest and Range Experiment Station in Missoula, Montana. His trips into the back country became legend and he penetrated the deep wilderness that in time would bear his name.

In 1929, the FS established regulations that provided for protection of areas as "primitive" — they were known as the "L" regulations. Later, a new classification, the "U" regulations, was designed and three areas — the upper Sun River, Pentagon and upper South Fork of the Flathead were parts of this classification. By 1934, Marshall was in Washington, D.C. arguing, pleading and insisting on the preservation of wilderness within the system of forest management.

That same year, two men deeply interested in wild-land preservation were in the Sun River country studying the recovery of the area's elk herd. Sitting up late one night in a cabin on Cabin Creek up the Sun River's North Fork, these men talked of the need for wilderness to secure both land and elk. That night, these two, Bob Cooney, then with the FS, assigned to the Sun River elk herd and his mentor, Dr. Olas Murie, one of the founding fathers of the Wilderness Society then working for the U. S. Fish and Wildlife Service out of Jackson Hole, Wyoming, quietly put their shoulders to the wheel and helped make it roll. Marshall continued to advocate the principle of wilderness nationwide, and Cooney carried on in Montana, emphasizing the preservation of wildlife by protecting land. It was an agenda internal to government agencies, and it led to success.

Bob Marshall died in 1939 and in 1940 the three primitive areas were united into one Forest Service-classified wilderness and named in his honor. Cooney went to work for the Montana Fish and Game Department and continued working for wilderness and wildlife until his retirement and beyond — his shoulder still to the wheel.

In the 1940s recovery of the area's wildlife, particularly elk, provided the first crisis and initiated an era of broad public involvement in wildland/wildlife preservation. The growing elk herd was causing friction with private landowners along the Rocky Mountain Front. Cooney and Bruce Neal, one of the last mountain men, of Augusta, Montana, were trying to hold back the elk in the mountains away from private ground. They recognized that the elk needed a foothills winter range and turned to Montana's people. The man they found was Tom Messelt, Great Falls businessman, sportsman and first secretary of the Montana Wildlife Federation. Messelt knew peace had to be declared between hunters and ranchers if the problem were to be solved. From a railroad freight shipper, Messelt learned that a key rancher who had suffered elk damage was shipping cattle to Chicago and there was room for one more on the cattle train. Messelt climbed aboard the train and when he returned, he had an established rapport with Charles Willard of Augusta, for Willard, too, cared about elk, wildlife and the land.

Messelt organized the Sun River Conservation Council to work for resolution of the winter range dilemma. It was a citizen's group and included Al Riegel, and Jess Gleason representing, along with Messelt, sportsmen from Helena, Choteau and Great Falls. Livestock interests were represented by Willard, Carl Malone and Les Barrett.

The break came late in 1947 when an elderly rancher named Brucegard put his place up for sale. The adjoining Wortheimer ranch came up for sale at the same time, and together they would make an ideal winter elk range. They were proper places in the right spot. The only catch was to hold them; the Fish and Game Department had to put up a $10,000 down payment and they had but a few hours to do it or lose it to another buyer. Even in 1947, government couldn't move fast enough; the future hung by a thread.

Archie O'Claire, director of the Fish and Game Department, turned to the Sun River Conservation Council — again the people responded. In a magnanimous move for any time, Messelt, the sportsman, and Malone, the Choteau rancher, were equal to the need. They made the down payment, and the elk were given a winter home forever. Bruce Neal, who lived with the elk all those long winters, herding them back into the mountains, was installed as first game-range manager, and he could now welcome the Sun River herd to the first real winter home of their own since white men settled the Rocky Mountain Front.

Another chapter in rebuilding the Bob Marshall Country was completed, and perhaps for the first time its authors were hunters, ranchers and a host of Montana people who simply cared. A new pattern was clearly emerging in the history of this land. It was a pattern of public support for the preservation of cherished values, wild places and animals living free. It was the first seed of a movement still growing in intensity. This seedling, barely sprouting, did not have long to wait before another challenge was issued.

In the late 1920s, a small storage reservoir, Gibson Dam, and a diversion dam downstream on the Sun River were built in Sun River Canyon. Ironically, the storage dam

The meeting to form the organization called the Citizens for the Great Bear Wilderness. Photo taken in the parking lot of Trixie's Saloon at Ovando, Montana. Meeting date March 12, 1977. Dale Burke photo.

Left, a 1965 field trip of the Montana Wilderness Association on Sun Butte, near site of proposed Sun Butte Dam. Bob Cooney photo.

Henry Loble of Helena camped below Mt. Wright, looking at the north face of Mt. Lockhart. Rick Graetz photo.

blocked the primitive access to upper Sun River and ended for all practical purposes livestock grazing and cutting for railroad ties in the back country.

By 1950, the Bureau of Reclamation advanced plans for another dam and more development that would take more land, block elk migration routes, flood bighorn sheep winter ranges and elk calving areas. The proposal was known as Upper Sun Butte Dam to be located between Sun Butte and Sheep Reef. The challenge was quickly answered by sportsmen, dude ranchers, outfitters, the Montana Fish and Game Department, and others. The threat quickly subsided, but only momentarily.

In 1953, the first in a series of floods swept the country. Other floods would recur in 1964 and 1975. The '53 flood brought the Bureau of Reclamation out in full force. The force was met head-on. Again, Messelt, Cooney and a new, young professional named Nels Thoreson of the Montana Fish and Game Department answered the call. Two even larger dams were now on the agenda. One, Lower Sun Butte at the confluence of the North and South Fork of the Sun River, the other a giant at the mouth of Sun River Canyon.

About that time the Montana Wilderness Association was formed with Dr. John Montagne and Ken and Florence Baldwin, all of Bozeman, as leading advocates for protecting Sun River Canyon and the wilderness beyond. The Montana Wildlife Federation was the dominant sportsman's group and Don Aldrich of Missoula was its prominent spokesman. The Cascade County Sportsmen's Association, often at odds with other groups over elk management, joined the alliance to save Sun River Canyon, and the Bureau of Reclamation soon retreated to await the next flood.

Mrs. Frances Allen, owner of the K-L dude ranch at the head of Gibson reservoir, was a most eloquent spokesperson during the dam battles. On her death, her estate created the Allen Foundation. The foundation to this day makes contributions to the preservation of the Sun River Canyon and the wildlife of her country.

During the dam battles of the 1950s, the Wilderness Society took an active interest in the issue — in 1954, Bob Cooney and Bruce Neal packed its Board of Directors to the Chinese Wall. Among those on the trip were Sig Olsen and his wife and old friends of the area Dr. Olas Murie and his wife Mardy, as well as two of Bob Marshall's brothers, George and Jim.

In 1964 another flood gave the Bureau of Reclamation new life, but again the people united against them; the conservationists remained clearly dominant. The Wilderness Act was passed by the Congress, the Bob Marshall was at that point formally wilderness, and the dam building threats of the 1960s passed into history on the Sun River.

About the same time, in the country to the north, the same problems plagued the Middle Fork of the Flathead and a whole new conservation constituency formed to defend the wild lands and waters of that area. Its leaders, Dr. Loren Kreck of Columbia Falls, Dr. John Craighead, the noted grizzly bear expert, who also developed a wild-rivers concept, and others formed a solid nucleus of leadership that eventually grew into a constituency for the Great Bear Wilderness.

With subsidence of the dam builders' threat, it was clear that the core of the country, the Bob Marshall Wilderness, was solid. The people now looked to extending wilderness protection to adjacent wild lands becoming vulnerable to surging commodity demands and a changing Forest Service philosophy.

The first blatant evidence of a changing Forest Service philosophy that aroused conservationists occurred in the Bunker Creek drainage. Bunker Creek, a tributary of the South Fork of the Flathead, was known to Kalispell sportsmen. It was elk, goat and grizzly country. The streams were important for bull trout and westslope cutthroat trout. It was also timber country and the Forest Service was after timber. Leaders emerged to contest the federal commodity merchants. It was a bitter battle, fought before any environmental laws were enacted, fought before the public was guaranteed access to federal decision making. It was a tough time, but the leaders who emerged were also tough. Clif Merritt and Dallas Eklund were state employment agency workers who came to the defense of Bunker Creek. Bob Sikes and Forrest Rockwood, both Kalispell attorneys, joined the fray. They were people whose names would continue to emerge as issue after issue was faced in and around the Bob Marshall Country. The battle was bitter and Bunker Creek fell to the bulldozer and chainsaw. The conservationists would rise to fight another day, Bunker Creek would never be forgotten.

First on people's agenda was the Lincoln back country, an area long a wilderness land, managed as a wilderness by the Forest Service, but without formal recognition as wilderness by Congress. In 1947, the Forest Service conducted "show me" trips into the country to convince influential citizens of the need for preservation. A Forest Service employee, Donald A. Roos, later said his instructions were to "sell these men on the beauty and solitude of the back country, to show them a part of the country and solitude of the back country, to show them a part of the country that was as God made it; unspoiled, quiet." The same person, Roos of Lincoln, Montana, testified that it was not until the mid-1960s that things changed. That change became evident in 1968 when the Forest Service revealed plans to develop the Lincoln back country, and Montana people responded in an awesome protest.

The Forest Service plan was titled "The Blackfoot-Sun River Divide Area, Management for People." The plan called for a scenic road crossing the Continental Divide southeast of Scapegoat Mountain, logging roads, campgrounds, logging 25 percent of the area, and winter recreation vehicle use. The opposition was led by two men of remarkable perception and determination — Cecil Garland, a Lincoln businessman and Tom "Hobnail" Edwards, a guide and outfitter. Garland quickly established himself as a dominant force in the Lincoln Scapegoat issue and subsequently went on to other conservation causes.

Garland came from the Smokey Mountains of Tennessee and North Carolina, a part of Appalachia. On September 23, 1968, in testimony before the Subcommittee on Public Lands of the Committee on Interior and Insular Affairs of the United States Senate, he told best what moves people who love wild land, what moved him:

"Senator Burdick, Senator Metcalf, and ladies and gentlemen: Fifteen years ago, when I first brought my family to the community of Lincoln, I was told of a great wild country to the north known as the Back Country. They told me with awe in their voices of places called Ringeye, Scotty Creek, Lost Pony, Red Mountain, the East Fork, the North Fork, Parker Lake, Meadow Lake, the Twin Lakes and an almost unworldly country called Scapegoat and Half Moon Park.

"I longed to see that country, to know its wild beauty, to catch its fish, to hunt its game, and to climb its mountains.

"Unusually wonderful, it was then, when the time came to pack our camp and move away from roads that led back to that world we call civilization.

"We camped that first night on a small bench above Ringeye Falls. Taking down our tent from an old frame that the pack rats were using for a home, we made a secure camp, cooked our supper, fed our stock, and then turned our complete thoughts to our whereabouts.

"We took from our duffle an old reed elk bugle and as the chill air fell with the sun we shattered the calm of that September evening with a blast from our elk call. Then almost as by magic, above us on Red Mountain a bull elk bugled his challenge that this was his home. All through the frosty fall air the calls echoed back and forth and I knew that I had found wilderness.

"I would not sleep that night for I was trying to convince myself that this was really so; that there was wild country like this left and that somehow I had found it. But all was not at peace in my heart for I knew that someday, for some unknown reason, man would try to destroy this country, as man had altered and destroyed before.

"That night I made a vow, that whatever the cost for whatever the reason, I would do all that I could to keep this country as wild as I had found it."

Cecil Garland kept the faith.

Tom Edwards, at the same hearing, put it this way:

"I am Tom Edwards, of Ovando, Montana. I have owned and operated the Whitetail Ranch continuously since 1937. My sole income comes from outfitting into the Lincoln-Scapegoat back country and the Bob Marshall Wilderness areas. For over a quarter of a century I have virtually lived in these areas, especially the Lincoln-Scapegoat back country, from Decoration Day to Thanksgiving. I have been privileged to take guests from all over the United States and some from foreign lands into every crook and cranny of this marvelous wilderness. I love the high country and alpine meadows with a passion — it restores my soul and into this land of spiritual strength I have been privileged to guide over the years literally thousands of people, the old, many past 70, the young, the poor, the rich, the great, and small people like myself. I have harvested a resource of the forest of most importance. No one word will suffice but to explain this resource let us call it the 'hush' of the land."

After Garland's and Edward's testimony the hearing turned into a rout; the people had their shoulders to the wheel. The procession of witnesses was impressive, and the wheel did roll. "Buff" Hultman, president of the Montana Wilderness Association; the Baldwins from Bozeman representing the Federation of Western Outdoor Clubs; Don Aldrich of the Montana Wildlife Federation; Dr. Clancy Gordon, president of Western Montana Scientists Committee for Public Information; Loren Kreck of Columbia Falls; Clif Merritt now of the Wilderness Society; Doris Milner, wildland advocate of Hamilton, Montana. The list could go on and on.

Before it was finished, three men who either were or would be governor of Montana testified in favor of wilderness — Tim Babcock, incumbent governor; Forrest Anderson, then attorney general; and Tom Judge, then a state senator. Harry Mitchell, a state senator from Great Falls, was a leading wilderness advocate and was responsible for getting 18 of his state senate colleagues to back wilderness classification.

As might be expected, those favoring commodity exploitation raised their voices in objection, but it was a whisper scarcely heard above the chorus of people demanding maximum protection — wilderness classification.

Although the day clearly belonged to the conservationists formal classification was still four years away. Four years of maneuvering through the maze of Washington, D.C. and back time and time again. In the U. S. Senate, Lee Metcalf was the people's champion. Over in the House, Western District Congressman Arnold Olsen laid the groundwork that eventually led to success in that chamber. Conservationists recall Olsen as always helpful and constantly supportive of preserving the area. In 1972 the Lincoln-Scapegoat was added to wilderness, anchoring the south end of a fantastic land.

To the north, the land lay vulnerable. Between the Bob Marshall and Glacier National Park, a wild, unprotected land and river would soon become a hotly contested terrain. The river, the Middle Fork of the Flathead, had seen contests before. In the 1950s the federal dam builders advanced a dam known as Spruce Park for the Middle Fork. Local conservationists, led by Dallas Eklund, Leland Schoonover, and Clif Merritt, as well as Archie O'Claire and Bob Cooney of the Fish and Game Department, never let it get off the ground.

Preservation of the Middle Fork and a vast portion of its watershed, the Great Bear, escalated into an intense and ultimately bitter struggle. The river itself was designated for study when Congress passed the National Wild and Scenic Rivers Act in 1969. The Forest Service conducted the mandated study and with overwhelming public support recommended the upper Middle Fork be "wild" — the most stringent classification option open to them. Before the end of 1976, Congress agreed, and a major victory was achieved. Key players in the campaign were Dr. John Craighead who pioneered the wild and scenic river concept; Dale Burk, outdoor writer and reporter for the dominant newspaper in western Montana, the *Missoulian;* Dr. Loren Kreck of Columbia Falls, and Bigfork residents Rick Trembath and Frank Noise.

The victory celebration was short-lived, for the conservationists were well aware of the fact that the Wild and Scenic Rivers Act gave little, if any, protection to the watershed that gives birth to the quality of wild waters. They knew full well that the bigger battle for the uplands, the Great Bear Wilderness, lay ahead and it would indeed be an intense struggle.

The Great Bear Wilderness proposal was not new. The obvious wild-land qualities caused a sportsmen's group in Kalispell to advocate its addition to the Bob Marshall in the mid-1950s. The Forest Service turned that request down. For the moment, land management in the Middle Fork slipped into limbo.

With conclusion of the Lincoln-Scapegoat classification battle to the south, it was obvious that the Forest Service would in the future be adverse to classifying land as wilderness. Their ill-conceived management plan for Lincoln's back country served only to galvanize a level of public support for wilderness that overwhelmingly carried the issue. Having learned from that relatively "up-front" approach, a new strategy was evident when it came time to engage the issue of the Great Bear.

The veterans of the battle to protect the river, working with a number of conservation groups, succeeded in getting a state legislative resolution passed asking that the area be protected. Ignoring, or at least taking no visible heed of the resolution, the Forest Service simply started selling trees, building roads and making plans to generally level the trees in the drainage. It was a time before the National Environmental Policy Act existed and public disclosure was primarily by leaks and dogged, hard-nosed snooping by people determined to pry off the lid and see just what was in store for the public land. Reporter Burk was masterful in his exposure of Forest Service plans for leveling the Great Bear and as a result, public response once again reached a new pinnacle.

Just how Burk became involved is a classic tale that demonstrates how a chain reaction among people who care can lead to success. An outfitter named Smoke Elser thought what the country needed was publicity and packed Lloyd Shermer, publisher of the Lee Newspaper chain in Montana, into the Great Bear. Shermer was so impressed that he called Burk from the first telephone he could find, Essex telephone station number one. He told Burk, "I want you in here next week to do a story about this, to save the Middle Fork of the Flathead." A week later Burk, working as a hand in Smoke Elser's outfit, packed a group of people into the country, some of whom were interested in the area's timber resource. It was set up for the local Forest Forest supervisor to ride in and lay out his development plans. The night the forester spoke Burk had his story, the people had the truth and the Great Bear had an advocate.

A core of conservationists recruited on Bunker Creek, seasoned on the river classification issue and now informed by Burk, soon recruited an aggressive constituency that rallied to the Great Bear. The first organizational meeting was held at Trixie's Bar in Ovando, Montana. Present at that meeting was a representative group of the rapidly swelling ranks of people willing to make a commitment for wild-land preservation. The group included: Phil Tawney, Tom Horabick, Bill Cunningham, Loren Kreck, Smoke Elser, Chris Roholt, Gene Sentz, Arlo Skari, Carly McCawley, Don Marble, Jean Warren, Beth Williams, Bob Anderson, Dallas Eklund, Doris Milner, Jim Posewitz, Bill Bishop, Rick Trembath, Rod Barkley, Dale Burk, and Bonnie Horbick.

The real giant of the Great Bear campaign was without doubt Montana's U. S. Senator, Lee Metcalf. Metcalf's recruitment to the cause of the Great Bear was quite casual. In the final days of the Lincoln-Scapegoat classification process Cecil Garland and Dale Burk were in Washington, D.C. to testify on the legislation. Talking with Garland on the possibility of taking on the Great Bear next, Burk was told, "You'll never get the Great Bear, it's the wrong wilderness at the wrong time." Undissuaded, Burk walked to the Senate office building and knocked on Lee Metcalf's door. After interviewing the Senator on another matter Burk asked, "I would like you to carry a cause on the Great Bear Wilderness." Burk remembers the Senator's response this way: "He said 'I'll do it,' never anything other than that, just I'll do it." Senator Metcalf seized the reins and it was only a matter of time before the Forest Service rush to alter and compromise the land was halted and wilderness classification was achieved for the Great Bear in 1978.

The pieces were finally in place, the land and its advocates rested in quiet celebration. The 1980s lay ahead.

Perhaps it is in the nature of the land; perhaps it is in the nature of man; perhaps it is just simply that this place is such a treasure it must be earned and fought for to be appreciated, but peace was not to last. No sooner had the main pieces been put together than pressure to begin tearing apart what had just been completed thrust itself across the land. Oil, gas, energy — the irresistible force of our industrialized culture could not wait to test its strength against the wild country and its band of advocates. Propelled by a series of energy "crises" and encouraged by the rhetoric of the Secretary of the Interior James Watt, the energy industry wanted access to the wilderness. First were seismic applications and lease applications to be debated and struggled over. Again and now in predictable pattern, the Montana conservationists rushed to the barricades. Organizations popped up overnight, coalitions developed — most important, leaders emerged. Missoula veterinarian Jim Brogger of the Backcountry Horsemen led the specifically created Bob Marshall Alliance in the defense of the Bob Marshall country. People like Bill Cunningham of Helena, Arnold Bolle of Missoula, and Bill Bishop of Polson, were seasoned and sophisticated advocates from the Montana Wilderness Association. Smoke Elser, Chuck Blixrud, and Max Barker anchored the outfitters securely in the battle. Bud Moore, retired forester of Swan Lake, and Bob Cooney brought the wisdom, reason and credibility earned over almost a half century of experience; George Engler, the savvy of a sensitive retired forester who knew how the system worked added still another dimension. These people and many other veterans provided the fuel for the battle and the new legions added the fire. New names and faces quickly lined up for counting — Hank Fischer of Missoula; Ed Madej, Rosemary Rowe of Helena; Joan Montagne of Bozeman, and many more.

The first salvo was a seismic permit and when the dust settled, Tom Coston, regional forester, denied the application. Still, seismic helicopters swarmed like angry bees around the wilderness boundary and applications for leasing within the three wilderness areas grew to cover virtually the entire land mass. While the debate raged in Montana, the issue quickly escalated to Washington, D.C. and became a test of strength and determination between Congress and Interior Secretary Watt. The wilderness was well represented by Montana's Western District Congressman Pat Williams, who proved to be nothing short of an angry silvertip when it came to the Bob Marshall and its defense. He led the fight with effective withdrawal resolutions, amendments and direct legislative action — always one effective step ahead of those who would seize an advantage and press a claim on the wilderness. With every plaintive cry that we must develop every conceivable energy resource, his response was simple, swift, certain and effective. "No, not here you don't," and he made it stick. In less than a year Pat Williams made a mark whose impact is sure to last for generations.

There were others, people like Les Pengelly, wildlife professor, Eldon and Liz Smith, educators and advocates, always close to every issue, preparing testimony, training and helping new advocates. The important thing is there was always someone.

So it is with the people who secured and now defend the Bob Marshall country. There is always a leader stepping forward, always a giant to stand in any tempest, always a midnight volunteer to stuff the envelopes. The wild land makes no distinction, it needs them all and rewards them equally.

It is impossible to predict the next threats to assail this land now preserved. History has taught us there will be an endless succession. History also attests that no challenge will go unanswered — not ever. Big oil can't have it, the chain saw can't scar it. It is the Sistine Chapel of the commons and the people say, let it be, let it be.

Names of the Bob Marshall

compiled by Rick Graetz

Alice Creek named for Alice Cox who died at an early age; family homesteaded in the area.

Arsenic Mountain Arsenic Creek named by early-day settlers because of odor of the creek. And water never freezes.

Baptiste Creek & Mountain are named for Felix Baptiste; some knew him as Baptiste Zeroyal. He was an early-day trapper and was instrumental in naming Spotted Bear. He is buried near his cabin on Hoke Creek. Felix Creek is also named for Baptiste.

Bartlett Creek & Mountain are named for a Forest Service employee.

Belton is named for James Belton, early trapper.

Benchmark named by original surveyors in the early '20s for the section-line benchmarks in the immediate area.

Benchmark Creek from U.S. Geological Survey benchmark established in 1900 on the north bank of the creek.

Big Bull Creek & Mountain are named for a trail foreman of 1914.

Big George Gulch named for early homesteader, trapper, and ladies' man, Big George Mathews.

Biggs Creek named after Charles Biggs who in about 1866 cut railroad ties along the North Fork Sun River.

Bloody Hill named for an incident involving a Forest Service mule that bucked off a pack, including a cross cut saw. The mule became entangled in the saw and was badly cut up. Another story about the origin of this name involves a battle between Flathead and Blackfeet Indians. The Blackfeet nearly wiped out a Flathead hunting party at this site. There is no historical evidence of the fight.

Bruce Creek is named for Flathead National Forest Supervisor Donald Bruce (1914-1915). When Bruce was married, a large branch of this creek was named Addition Creek. When the Bruces' first child was born, a large fork of Addition Creek was named Little Creek.

Bum Shot Mountain named for local hunting party. Two members of the party ran into small herd of elk and emptied their rifles without drawing blood.

Bunker Creek named for Page S. Bunker, Flathead National Forest Supervisor, 1905-1913.

Calbick Creek is named for Allen Calbick, early ranger.

Clack Creek is named for Jack Clack, early Assistant Supervisor of the Flathead.

Cooney Creek and Mountain named for an outlaw.

Coram is named for William Coram, early-day Kalispell timberman.

Creeks in the Lower South Fork — Mazie, Anna, Pearl, Goldie, Emma, Flossie, Elya, Maggie, Mamie, Doris and others — were named for girls U.S.G.S. men met in town.

Danaher Creek & Mountain are named for Thomas Danaher, early Ranger who homesteaded here in 1898. His homestead was in what is now the Bob Marshall Wilderness.

Danaher River and Meadows also named for Thomas Danaher, homesteader; some old horse drawn hay equipment remains in Danaher meadow.

Dean Ridge, Dean Creek & Dean Lake are named for Richard Dean, early Ranger in the area (1913-1914).

Dearborn River "This handsome bold and clear stream we named in honor of the Secretary of War calling it the Dearborn's River." Capt. Meriwether Lewis, July 18, 1805.

Dirty Face Creek is named for "Dirty Face" McDonald, early trapper and prospector.

Flathead River named for a group of Salish-speaking Indians living in the area. The group was called Flathead by other local Indian groups, in the belief that Flatheads pressed the heads of their young to flatten them. The Flatheads say the belief is false.

Gates Park named after homesteader named Cates. The name was misspelled.

Gibson Reservoir named for Paris Gibson, founder of Great Falls.

Gordon Creek & Doctor Lake are named for Dr. Gordon, who established the Gordon Ranch near Holland Lake.

Great Bear Creek & Mountain were named by Senator Penrose of Pennsylvania.

Great Northern Mountain named for Great Northern Railroad.

Grimsley Creek & Grimsley Park are named for "Chick" Grimsley, early-day trapper and guide. Grimsley came from Texas with a trail herd as a boy and located near the Blackfoot Indian Agency. He came into the Middle Fork in 1896.

Hahn Creek misspelled from the name of Frank D. Haun, an early day forester.

Hahn Peak named for Tom Hahn, who trapped in the area in 1908.

Hannan Gulch Jim Hannan, local homesteader, operated a station for horse thieves on the Oregon Trail, also liked neighbors' beef steak. Local cattlemen left a hangsman's noose on a tree near Hannan's house (in what is now Hannan's Gulch) and put several bullet holes in his front door. After that, Hannan was never seen in the area again. The bullet holes were still in the door when the cabin became a Ranger Station.

Hart Creek & Hart Basin are named for Evert Hart, Forest Service employee who built the Limestone and Black Bear cabins in 1925.

Headquarters Pass Headquarters Creek was originally named Tie Hacker Creek because of many cabins built by tie hackers (railroad tie cutters) in the area. It later became a headquarters for tie hackers, hence the name headquarters.

Hoke Creek is named for Ranger Ellis B. Hoke.

Holbrook Creek & Mountain are named for Ranger Fred Holbrook. A Mormon, Holbrook was raised by Brigham Young's favorite wife, Amelia.

Holland Lake named for the first settler, B.B. Holland.

Hungry Horse got its name because two horses became lost in the area and nearly starved.

Koessler Lake named after Doctor Koessler.

Logan Creek is named for Sidney M. Logan, who worked mining claims in this area.

Marshall Creek is named for a trapper. He died about 1918.

Monture Creek named for George Montour, a half-breed who was killed by Indians near the mouth of the North Fork of the Blackfoot River.

Morrell Creek named after Fred Morrell, early-day ranger.

Mortimer Gulch named for Johnnie Mortimer, homesteader, recluse, bachelor.

Moser Mountain named after early-day Forest Supervisor headquarterd at Ovando.

Mt. Bradley & Bradley Creek are named for Richard Bradley, early-day Forest Ranger in the area.

Mt. Drewyer phonetic spelling honoring George Drouillard, interpreter and hunter for the Lewis and Clark expedition.

Mt. Field misspelled from the name of Joseph and Reuben Fields, brothers from Kentucky shown on the Lewis and Clark Expedition roll.

Mt. Forester is named for W.J. Forester, member of a U.S.G.S. crew of 1914.

Mt. Frazier named after Robert Frazier, member of the Lewis and Clark expedition.

Mt. Furlong is named for James Furlong, early trapper and prospector. He worked for the Great Northern from 1900 to 1924.

Mount Liebig named for Frank Liebig. He trained in Germany as a forester and camed to the Flathead area at the turn of the century. His first Ranger District assignment was in 1901 in what is now Glacier National Park.

Mount Lockhart named for former Lewis and Clark National Forest Supervisor, killed by a horse at the old cabin at the Base of Mount Lockhart.

Mt. Patrick Gass after Patrick Gass, a member of Lewis and Clark Expedition.

Mt. Werner named after Willard Werner a member of the Lewis and Clark expedition.

Mount Wright Capt. Wright was in charge of tie and wood cutting operations for the Government at the head of Teton River in 1908.

Murphy Flats, between Holbrook and Salmon Forks, is named for Joe Murphy, outfitter from Ovando. He and his family have used this area as a campsite since 1919.

Neil Creek near Reclamation Flats named after Bruce Neal.

Phil Creek named for Phillip Clack, former Ranger, and brother of former Assistant Supervisor Jack Clack.

Renshaw Mountain Renshaw was an early-day tie hacker.

Rogers Pass named for Milwaukee railroad surveyor who surveyed the area.

Scapegoat Mountain USGS surveyor (Chapman), working in the area in 1897-1900, gave the peak the name Scapegoat after he had difficulty surveying the area.

Scarface Mountain named for Piegan Indian God.

Schafer Meadows & Schafer Creek are named for William Schafer, a trapper. His headquarters cabin was at Schafer Meadow. He was found dead in his cabin in 1908. Circumstances indicated he had been robbed. He was buried on Morrison Creek near the mouth of Lodgepole Creek.

Shaw Creek & Mountain are named for Ezra Shaw, early-day ranger at Seeley Lake.

Shields Creek & Mountain are named for Thomas Shields, Great Northern Railroad telegraph operator and Essex postmaster. Marion Lake is named for his daughter; and Almeda Lake, for his wife.

Slippery Bill Mountain & Morrison Creek are named for William H. Morrison, early-day trapper and forest ranger. He had squatter's rights on 160 acres at Summit, where he lived by his wits until he died in Kalispell in March 1932.

Sock Lake A trail and fire crew were camped at the head of Red Shale Creek while working on a fire on Moonlight Peak in the '20s. They visited the lake to "mop up" and found socks hanging in the trees, thus the name.

Spotted Bear is one of the oldest known names in the Flathead National Forest. This name has been attached to a river, a mountain, and a Forest Service Ranger Station in the South Fork area. The story of how this name originated was related to Charlie Shaw by the late Harry Wilson, one of the more rugged individuals who trapped and prospected for a living in this country. It was in the winter of 1933-34. Wilson invited Ranger Albert Campbell and Shaw to spend the night in Wilson's cabin on Sullivan Creek. They were making a big-game study in the area. During the evening, Harry told them his version of how the name Spotted Bear came into being. He said he had never heard any story to the contrary. Wilson explained that back in about 1861, two prosperous California miners were looking for a guide to pack them through the mountains to the east side of the Continental Divide. Inquiring at the Hudson Bay Trading Post at Salish for a good guide, they were referred to Baptiste Zeroyal, better known as Felix Baptiste or just Baptiste. Few men in those days were more familiar with this wilderness area than Baptiste. Because the Blackfeet Indians were more or less perpetually on the warpath at that time, Baptiste decided the best route to travel was up the South Fork and Spotted Bear Rivers and down Sun River. One day on the journey, while camped near the mouth of the Spotted Bear River, they saw a black bear with an unusual amount of white on its breast and underside. Thus, the name Spotted Bear was created.

Spotted Eagle Mountain named for one of the Blackfeet Indian chiefs who signed 1895 treaty that ceded the area to the Government.

Sullivan Creek is named for a former Spotted Bear District Ranger, John Sullivan.

Swan Range and River named for the large number of trumpeter swans in the area.

Two Medicine River named by Blackfeet Indians. The Indians believed the high mountains on the eastern edge of Glacier Park had spiritual powers. The two forks of the Two Medicine River drain this area, thus the name Two Medicine or Big Medicine.

Waldbillig Mountain, near the head of Gordon Creek on the Big Prairie District, is named for a Forest Service employee and game warden. About 1906, while attempting to arrest a group of Flathead Indians caught violating game laws in the Pendant Creek area, he was killed by the Indians. Another game warden by the name of Morgan from Ovando came in and packed out the body. The Indians fled. No one was ever convicted for this murder.

Wall Creek is named for Chet Wall, Forest Service employee.

White River is named for Steward Edward White, famous author.

Youngs Creek named after Charles "Kid" Young who trapped and worked for the Forest Service at the turn of the century.

An autumn scene at Hannan Gulch. Bill Lancaster photo.

Left top: The start of the South Fork of the Flathead River at the confluence of Youngs Creek and the Danaher River. C.B. Rich - Double Arrow Ranch photo.

Left bottom: Lick Lake and the head of Lick Creek in the Swan Range. C.B. Rich - Double Arrow Ranch photo.

Above: Three Sisters Peaks and head of Baldy Bear Creek. U.S. Forest Service photo.

The "Arsenic Creek Cabins" just outside the wilderness boundary. Rick Graetz photo.

The Chinese Wall from above Moose Creek. Rick Graetz photo.

West Fork of the South Fork of the Sun River. Rick Graetz photo.

Prairie Reef. Rick Graetz photo.

139

North face of Rocky Mountain peak from below Headquarters Pass. Rick Graetz photo.

Conclusion
and
Acknowledgements

by Rick Graetz

This then is the story of the Bob Marshall Country. It is by no means complete. To be sure, one could dig for many hours into the historical background of the area for more colorful tales and perhaps the origin of a few more of the names. Indeed, I hope that as people read this book, they might send me suggestions of historical notes that should be included in any possible revised editions.

It should be emphasized again that this is a book describing wilderness, a very special place that requires great care upon the part of each visitor. Use of this wild country is increasing annually and more human impact is becoming evident. It is for this reason that use of the Bob Marshall must be spread out and directed away from the most frequently used places. It is also paramount that users begin practicing low-impact camping. For instance, when a fire is necessary, it is best to dig a pit, saving the sod, and then scattering the ashes over a wide area and replanting and watering the sod. Areas prone to muddiness should be avoided when they are wet. Camping away from lakes or grassy banks along stream beds is another good idea. The use of commercially made tents is more desirable from an impact standpoint than cutting poles for tents.

The Forest Service, the agency charged with managing these wilderness lands, confronts the undesirable task of putting more and more restrictions on users. Restrictions are now in effect on the number of people who may be part of a commercial party. No new outfitter permits are being granted. Many of the Forest Service personnel who are in the field each summer are trying to reach as many people as possible to instruct them in low-impact camping and other concerns.

The commercial outfitters have been using this land for a long time. At one time they far outnumbered private parties. However, now they are being outnumbered by users who visit the land free of charge, while the outfitters must pay ever-increasing fees. Yet it is the outfitters who are most dedicated to the future well-being of the country. Many of them are attempting to protect and add land to the Bob Marshall complex. Often they are unfairly blamed for messes left behind by private groups.

Not only must the Forest Service contend with ways to minimize impact, but it is also faced with requests from exploitation interests such as oil and gas developers who would destroy the wilderness qualities of the area. In the case of the exploitation versus wilderness-protection conflicts, public sentiment has been a strong determinant in deciding the land-use conflicts in favor of wild values. But the problem of increasing recreational use remains to be solved by the land managers. Whatever solutions they come up with are not going to satisfy everybody.

The Forest Service is attacked from all sides, in places even in this book. But it is important to note, especially on the local level, that there are many good, dedicated people in the Forest Service who care about wilderness and are committed to what they are doing in an unselfish way. I've been privileged to meet outstanding district rangers, wilderness rangers and administrators in the Region 1 Headquarters in Missoula. These people have been most helpful to me, and I have observed their concern for wilderness when I met them in the back country.

In putting this book together, I am most grateful for the help received from personnel in the Forest Service. Names that come to mind now are Jud Moore, Ray Karr, Lloyd Swanger, Ray Mills, Steve Solem, Betty Chamberlain, Dale Gorman, Cynthia Manning Hamlett, Milo McLeod and Gary McLean.

And Grayson Cordell, meteorologist in charge of the National Weather Service in Helena, Montana, was a great help in putting together the weather section. Thanks also to his fellow weather forecasters in Helena: Max Baumgartner, Dave Taylor, Jack Poppe, Darrell Pruett and Harold Crowl for all the information they supplied to me in terms of expected weather as I set out on my various Bob Marshall trips.

Many other people, who have either been associated with the Forest Service.or who know the country, have also helped. They are Bob Cooney, C.B. Rich, Al and Mildred Chaffin, Joe White, Max Barker, Roland Cheek, Chuck Blixrud and others.

A special thanks is also in order to Mark Thompson, Director of Publications for MONTANA MAGAZINE, who helped with much of the editing and planning of the book. Dave Alt, Jim Posewitz and Bob Cooney are to be thanked for their great contributions, as are Bill Lancaster, Jeff Strickler and Gus Wolfe for their photos.

Then there is my wife Kristine, son Todd and daughter Kara, who were understanding in my absence for field work. Thanks to them.

And last I am most grateful to one very special person who has dedicated much of his life to the preservation of wild country, a man respected not only by those who agree with him, but also by the people who oppose him, and a brilliant person with incredible energy. I speak of William "Wild Bill" Cunningham of Helena, Montana.

About The Writers

Rick Graetz of Helena is the publisher of MONTANA MAGAZINE and the Montana Geographic Series, and a partner in High Country Adventures, a mountaineering and backpacking guide service. He has been a licensed guide for more than 10 years. Graetz has climbed and hiked through North and South America and in Asia. His photographs and articles have appeared in many national publications. With his son Todd, and many friends and clients, he has hiked more than 2,000 miles in the Bob Marshall Country. Rick Graetz has had leadership positions in numerous local, state and national civic and citizen organizations, including groups formed to protect the Bob Marshall Wilderness.

Bob Cooney was raised on a ranch near Canyon Ferry, east of Helena, Montana, and was graduated from the School of Forestry at the University of Montana in range and wildlife. For eight years he worked with the U.S. Forest Service as a ranger and wildlife specialist. Three of these years were spent on an elk study in the Bob Marshall Wilderness country. In 1940 he transferred to the Montana Fish and Game Department (now the Department of Fish, Wildlife and Parks), and for the next 25 years he was in charge of the Game Management Division. He aided in the development of a new Division in the Department, which incorporated Outdoor Recreation and Parks. One of his responsibilities was to conduct studies of wilderness areas and their relationship to wildlife. He also worked with the Wild and Scenic Rivers program. Bob retired in 1971 after 32 years with the Montana Department of Fish, Wildlife and Parks. Following retirement he spent three years in Denver managing the National Wilderness Society's trip program.

Jim Posewitz, Helena, holds both B.S. and M.S. degrees in fish and wildlife management from Montana State University. During his more than 23 years working for the Montana Department of Fish, Wildlife and Parks, Jim has directed much of his energy towards preservation of wild lands and rivers. He has received awards of recognition for his professional activities and for his work with citizen's organizations. Jim writes for government and private publications on the subjects of wildlife conservation and wild-land philosophy.

Dave Alt was graduated in 1961 from the University of Texas, Austin, with a Ph.D. in geology. He came to the University of Montana in 1965, and has taught geology there ever since. Dr. Alt has authored several books, including *Roadside Geology of the Northern Rockies*, a basic geology text book and a geology-oriented publication on Glacier National Park. He is the geology columnist for MONTANA MAGAZINE.

THE MONTANA GEOGRAPHIC SERIES

Editions of the Montana Geographic Series are published three times a year. Each book in the series has between 96 and 150 pages of the highest quality color photography of Montana. Books are authored especially for this series and make a prized collection.

As of this writing, the following titles have been released.

MONTANA MOUNTAIN RANGES

EASTERN MONTANA: A Portrait of the Land and Its People

MONTANA WILDLIFE

GLACIER COUNTRY: Montana's Glacier National Park

WESTERN MONTANA: A Portrait of the Land and Its People

GREATER YELLOWSTONE: The National Park and Adjacent Wildlands

BEARTOOTH COUNTRY: Montana's Absaroka and Beartooth Mountains

MONTANA'S MISSOURI RIVER

MONTANA'S EXPLORERS

MONTANA'S YELLOWSTONE RIVER

MONTANA'S INDIANS Yesterday and Today

MONTANA'S CONTINENTAL DIVIDE

EASTERN MONTANA'S MOUNTAIN RANGES: Islands on the Prairie

Two to three new books in the Montana Geographic Series are published each year. The books are available in bookstores, or through MONTANA MAGAZINE, Box 5630, Helena, MT 59604 — (406) 443-2842. For ordering information write to the above address and ask for information on the MONTANA GEOGRAPHIC SERIES.

MONTANA MAGAZINE

MONTANA MAGAZINE is published 6 times a year and has been acclaimed as one of the most beautiful and informative regional magazines in the nation. Each issue features regular sections on people, towns, geology, history, outdoor recreation, travel, wilderness, outdoor equipment and much more. And every edition features a center section of full-page color photos of Montana scenery and wildlife.

For subscription information or to order, write MONTANA MAGAZINE, P.O. Box 5630, Helena, Montana 59604.